Two Centuries of a Cumberland Village

Blennerhasset

Geoffrey Bremner

Bookcase

Acknowledgements

This book could not have been written without the help of a large number of people and I should like to record my grateful thanks to them all.

To Susan Dench, David Bowcock and the staff of the Carlisle Records Office for their unfailing helpfulness and patience in directing me to sources of information and enlightening me on the many areas where I was ignorant. To Dennis Perriam, who read through the draft typescript, put me right on some points and supplied much extra information drawn from his vast knowledge of local history.

Many people in the village gave up their time to talk to me and also lent me photographs and other documents. They are, in alphabetical order: Bill Atkinson, Brian Atkinson, Eileen Blair, Jean Bowe, Trish Bowe (for 'who was who' in the pub's recent history), Ada Brownrigg (who gave me a wealth of information about the past history of the village), John Carruthers, Andy and Louise Close-West (who supplied documents about Peare Tree House), Andy Curle (who talked to me about the mill), Maureen Graham, Anne Jones, Bruce Kemp, Dorothy Relph, John and Barbara Reynolds (for the results of their research into 4 Winder Cottages), Mike Richardson, Glenn Stamper (for lending me the deeds of The Grey Goat), Allyson Stevenson (the Head Teacher of the school, who lent me the school records, which were particularly valuable), Gordon Thompson, Peter Turner (for information and documents about sport in the village), Ted and Mary Winter (who were a mine of information about the history of the village).

The Story of a Cumbrian Village: Blennerhasset.
Copyright Geoffrey Bremner, 2006
ISBN 1904147194
First Edition 2006
Published by Bookcase, 19 Castle Street, Carlisle, CA3 8SY
01228 544560   www.bookscumbria.com

Contents

Blennerhasset as it appeared from the air in 1995. Baggrow is to the bottom of the picture.

4

Introduction

The title 'Two centuries of a Cumbrian Village' is not quite an accurate description of the contents of this book. The accurate, but far too cumbersome title should be The last two centuries and a number of mentions of the two before. This is because there is not much in the way of written records for the early history of villages in this part of Cumbria.

We know that Blennerhasset has existed for a very long time, with a variety of spellings and pronunciations. To pick out some of the more picturesque items from the list given in *The Place names of Cumberland*: Blenherseta; Blencherhayset; Blynroset and

Above:The village seen from the eastern side in about 1905. The two children are walking along the main road through the village. On the left, half of it visible, is seventeenth century Peare Tree House. The larger house on the left is the new manse, built in 1864 and in the centre is the one surviving older house of the row that originally stood there. On the right are Cross Cottages, then the property of Sir Wilfrid Lawson.

The signpost and war-memorial on the village green.

Blinrasset (the last quite closely resembling the local pronunciation of the present day). But there is no Domesday Book version of the name because that survey reached only as far as parts of south Cumbria.

According to *The Place Names of Cumberland*, 'hasset' is Old Norse, the language of the Vikings, and means a 'hay shieling' and the 'blenner' is Celtic, meaning a slope or mound. One can only suppose that the compilers had never taken the trouble to come and see the village for themselves. They would have been hard put to find any slopes in Blennerhasset, which is comfortably stretched out flat in the valley of the River Ellen. A more likely explanation can be found in a letter of 1933 from a Mr Fred Field of Edinburgh to the then Headmaster of Blennerhasset School, Mr Gaskarth. He thought that the village was probably founded during the Viking settlements in the tenth century. 'Hasset' would indeed mean 'hay shieling', but 'Blenner' was perhaps a Norse personal name and that

Present day Blennerhasset

of the original owner of the field.

As for the Blennerhasset family, the name first appears m records of about 1270 as 'de Blennerhasset', which suggests that they took their name from the village. The family had moved to Carlisle by 1388 when Alan de Blennerhasset was mayor of the city, and then in the mid-sixteenth century to Flimby Hall until the death of William Blennerhasset in 1772. The name does crop up in the area later than this, but by then most of the descendants had moved either to Norfolk or to Ireland. The name, or half of it, is preserved in the village of Blennerville, near Tralee, founded by Roland Blennerhasset. There is also a Blennerhassett, with two t's, in West Virginia, but the origin of this name is obscure. One English visitor was told that the name was probably native American so at least he was able to put his American informant right on that.

Long before the name Blennerhasset was thought of, there was a Roman settlement here, south of where the village now stands. Its site was discovered as a result of an aerial survey in 1984 on the land of Richard Tinniswood beside the River Ellen. The survey revealed a triple-ditch system with four gateways. It was quite an

Geese on the Green

extensive fort, about eight and a half acres, larger than any other found in Cumbria. Apart from the evidence from the air the only remains consist of shards of Samian ware, perhaps dating from the early second century AD[1]. The find is historically important because it proves that the Roman army did not by-pass the Lake District, as was previously believed. The only other evidence of the early history of the village can be found underneath the was memorial. Here there is an older foundation which must be that of the cross marked as such on the Ordnance Survey map. These crosses usually date back to Anglian or Norse times. They do not necessarily have any religious significance but often acted as waymarkers for travellers. This one may be really ancient or it may be a market cross dating from more recent times.

If the Domesday surveyors had ventured as far as North Cumberland we should have had some idea of the land under cultivation and the people who lived here in the eleventh century, as well, perhaps, as a mention of the Blennerhasset family. As it is, there is a certain amount of information about the successive owners

The bridge across the Ellen into Blennerhasset

The bridgr across the Ellen leading to Baggrow.

9

Above: A few of the many children that lived in Blennerhasset in the early part of the twentieth century.
Below: looking to the west of the village a hundred years ago.

Above; The Cobbler's shop in its prime.
Below: The west end of Cross cottages and houses facing on to the Green.

The School and the Master's House.

of the village and a little more detail when we reach the seventeenth century but nothing really comprehensive before the end of the eighteenth. For that reason this account will deal mainly with the past two hundred or so years with a mention from time to time of earlier events. What I have chosen to do, rather than attempt a full chronological history, is to select the aspects of the past which I have found interesting, significant, or just amusing, in the hope that they will interest others

Blennerhasset today is a small village as it has always been and there seems little likelihood of it ever growing much bigger, but one never knows. Most of its eighty or so houses lie round a village green, with a few more stretching along the roads to meet the agricultural land which surrounds it. A lot of people have heard of Blennerhasset. They will have noticed the rather unusual name on the signpost as they drive between Carlisle and Cockerrnouth. Few of those people will have taken the trouble to turn off the main road to see it, but it would have been worth their while. Seen from most angles it is a pleasant place.

Torpenhow Church

About a mile down a turning off the main road which runs north-east from Cockermouth to Carlisle, the village green stretches out to the left and the right, shaded by trees. Round it the houses are mostly fairly modest dwellings, but different enough in style to offer a pleasing variety. A little further down the road, on the far side of the green, is the small primary school, healthy and surviving despite the occasional rumour of closure. Opposite it is a shop which has seen better days. Above the door a plaque bears the information that it was founded by the philanthropist William Lawson (of whom more later) in 1867. Then comes the bridge across the River Ellen. enlivened by a colony of ducks and geese. A little further on and we find ourselves in the adjacent village of Baggrow

One thing the village lacks, has always lacked in fact, is a parish church. Anglican churchgoers had to trudge the two miles to Torpenhow (in the same parish) to attend services. For the many dissenters in the village a Congregational Chapel was built at the beginning of the eighteenth century and rebuilt in 1828. This has since become a private house and for any remaining worshippers

13

there is only the Evangelical Mission at the west end of the village, near the Village Hall. There is a pub though, the Grey Goat, actually down the road in Baggrow, just a few metres from where Blennerhasset ends, so both villages tend to treat it as their own.

Like most villages in the area, Blennerhasset has never become a commuter village. Although a fair number of its inhabitants do work in nearby towns such as Carlisle and Workmgton, there are enough people left to keep the place alive during the day. Nor has it been transformed into a haven for city dwellers seeking a second home for an occasional weekend of rural calm. Only a few miles south it's a different story for there are the lakes and fells of the Lake District (with correspondingly higher house prices) instead of the rolling farmland here, attractive enough, it's true, but perhaps not enough to compensate for the remote situation. So Blennerhasset has a representative population - the old. the middle-aged, the young and the very young the last of whom enjoy the rare privilege of being able to run straight out of their houses to play on the green.

Although the village has often known hard times there is evidence that it may have been a fairly prosperous place in the seventeenth century. Blennerhasset mill dates back at least to this period and is probably very much older and the village was one of four given permission to establish a market about 1661[1]. Some of the houses go back to the seventeenth century or beyond. Two of them have datestones from the later part of the century which might indicate that they were built then or else were partly rebuilt and improved at that date by more wealthy owners. The owners of one of the Winder houses (see later for more on these) kindly supplied me with the findings of their research into its history and these certainly point at least to the seventeenth-century, judging from the general layout and various details like fire beams, a spice cupboard, inglenooks and support beams. Such is the sparse information available about the earlier history of the village and we have to leap forward more than a century before any positive evidence can be seen.

14

When I began to investigate the history of the area in the archives at Carlisle Castle I was first led to the Lawson records. Sir Wilfrid Lawson (1829-1906) had by the end of the nineteenth century bought most of the land in Blennerhasset to add to his already vast estates and consequently gathered together the deeds relating to the ownership of the lands and dwellings. These have now found their way to the public archives, where they have been catalogued and summarized. What immediately becomes apparent is that much of the history of the village was decided by landowners who for the most part never lived here. Until well on into the nineteenth century one of the best forms of investment was in land which could be let to local farmers. Few people owned the homes they lived in or the land they cultivated.

There is a longstanding belief that the rural villages of England were static communities, their inhabitants living and dying without ever knowing much about the world around them, apart perhaps from a rare visit to the nearest market town. This belief was certainly held by George Eliot when she wrote in Silas Marner, 'To the peasants of old times (she is writing here about the beginning of the nineteenth century) the world outside their own direct experience was a region of vagueness and mystery to their untravelled thought, a state of wandering was a conception as dim as the winter life of the swallows that came back with the spring.' This may once have been true of Blennerhasset, but it is far from true of the time in the mid-nineteenth century when, thanks to the census, it becomes possible to get some idea of where people came from and how long they stayed.

The population census of 1851 is the first to tell us where people were born and it contains the startling information that hardly any of the inhabitants of Blennerhasset were actually born here, a fact which suggests that the village had had a shifting population for some time before that. People seem to have been constantly on the move, looking for work. John Curwen of Workington Hall, writing at the start of the nineteenth century, says 'The love of change is grown so prevalent, that few farm servants choose to remain above

The undermentioned Houses are situate within t...

		Municipal Ward		Urban Sanitary District		Town or Villag
...cipal Borough		of		of		of *Blenn...*

4 ES (Unin-habited J.) or (B.)	5 Number of rooms occupied if less than five	6 NAME and Surname of each Person	7 RELATION to Head of Family	8 CON-DITION as to Marriage	9 / 10 AGE last Birthday of Males / Females	PROFESS...
	2	George Rumney	Head	Wid	67	Far...
		Joseph do	GranSon	Single	24	
	3	James Carr	Head	Wid	70	Far...
		Jane do	Daug	Single	30	
		Robert Druggin	Boarder	Wid	26	Coa...
	4	James Iredale	Head	Mar	37	Offic...
		Esther do	Wife	do	34	
		John do	Son	Single	8	
		Robert do	do		2	
		Mary do	Daug		4	
		Margaret do	do		4 mnths	
		Esther Graham	Mother	Wid	67	
		edward Jeffers	Head	Mar	47	Cotton...
		Catherine do	Wife	do	47	
		George do	Son	Single	14	
		Mary do	do	do	15	
		John do	Son		11	
		Margaret Harrison	Head	Single	60	Dau...
		Thomas Mann	Head	Mar	86	
		Susannah do	Wife	do	75	
	4	Edward Harker	Head	Mar	55	Road...
		Catherine do	Wife	do	50	
		Edward do	Son	Single	24	
		Rachel do	Daug	do	14	
		Jane do	do		14	
		Ann Steel	Head	Wid	64	
		Joseph do	Son	Single	26	Sho...
		Sarah Ashcroft	Head	Wid	59	Far...

An extract from the 1891 census.

16

a year, or two, in the same place'[2]. Certainly William Wordsworth's sister Dorothy, writing her journals at the beginning of the century a bit further south in Grasmere, repeatedly talks of travellers calling at the house, on their way to find a job somewhere.

Although censuses began in 1801 and were carried out at ten-year intervals after that, the first few are of limited value, simply listing names and occupations, but the five censuses for the second half of the century (1851-1901) give ages, occupation, birthplace, and, in 1901, the total number of rooms in the house if less than five, which meant that 57 houses out of 95 in Blennerhasset were listed with two, three or four rooms. One thing that is missing in Blennerhasset's case is the exact location of the houses. There were no named streets or any other way of giving an address. To give some idea of population movement of those families living in the village in 1841, only about a dozen were still there in 1851 and at that time there were 41 houses, four of them empty. Some of these disappearances can be accounted for by deaths, but in most cases the people seem simply to have moved on. By 1891 hardly any of those who remained, or their descendants, were still there. The two great stayers, there in 1841 and still present in 1891, aged respectively 86 and 75, were Thomas Mann, master joiner and cartwright, and his wife, Susannah. But Thomas was not born in the village. In fact he seems uncertain of his birthplace, or else he had little respect for the accuracy of the census. At different times he gives his place of birth as Abbey Holm, Baggrow, Mealrigg and Holm Cultram. Susannah, though, seems actually to have been born in Blennerhasset, apart from one census return when she says it was Aspatria. The Manns had ten children most of whom seem to have survived into adulthood. The ninth, Jane Ann, born in 1852, married in 1882 John Blacklock, the father, himself a grocer, of the Joseph Blacklock who bought the 'People's Shop' from Sir Wilfrid Lawson. It was the one shop which still remained in the village until its unfortunate closure very recently.

In the earlier censuses we can see that most of the villagers had not in fact travelled very far from their places of birth, which were in the surrounding villages, rarely more than ten miles away. The exceptions were a few agricultural labourers who had made their way from Scotland, as also had Thomas Salmon, the Congregational minister, who must have lived in the house at the east end of the village, now known as The Old Manse, next door to the chapel. The first sign of a dramatic change came in 1871 when the first coalminers are listed, four in number, but the village was still mainly occupied, as it always had been, by farmers (5) and farmhands (42), this out of a total population of 280. By 1881 the character of Blennerhasset had changed dramatically. The number of farmhands had shrunk to little more than half of the 1871 figure and there were 30 workers in the pits as well as 13 more people employed on the surface. But this was not the end of the expansion. The high point came at the end of the century: in the 1891 census the figure for miners underground had risen to 50, with 14 more on the surface, while the number of farmhands was down to eight. After that numbers begin to fall, to 46 miners below ground and 15 above in the 1901 census.

We cannot know how the people of Blennerhasset reacted to the village being swamped, as it must have seemed, by miners, not to speak of a few workers on the new Carlisle to Maryport railway, but for the first time they had to grow accustomed to meeting with people who not only carried on a different trade but quite often came from some distance away. Most, it's true, were from North Cumberland, though drawn from a wider area than before. Some miners, however, had their origins in Devon, Warwickshire and Gloucestershire. Farmhands, too, were coming from far away, in several cases from Ireland. And the village must have seemed crowded: from 163 in 1841 the population had grown to 416 in 1891, while the number of inhabited houses had grown from 39 to 93. The village, not to speak of the school, must have been swarming with children: families with six, seven or eight children were not uncommon. Then, as the numbers of miners went down, so did the population of the village, with just over 380 in 1901, the latest census available to be seen in detail. The present population is about 200.

Occupations

Looking more closely at what people did for a living, the main source of knowledge before the census became available comes from the Militia Lists[3]. The militia goes back before medieval times and was created to act as a regional defence force. It lasted until 1907, when it was amalgamated into the Territorial Force, later to become the Territorial Army. Service was usually voluntary but in times of emergency it became compulsory. This was the case in the early nineteenth century during the Napoleonic Wars, when the threat of invasion by Bonaparte's forces was a very real one. The Militia Lists for Blennerhasset are available for this period. In 1807, for example, we have the list of 'all Persons between the Ages of eighteen and forty-five years in the township of Blennerhasset liable and not liable to serve in the Militia of the County of Cumberland'. In this list there were three yeomen (owners or tenants of a fair amount of land), eight husbandmen or servants in husbandry (agri-cultural workers), two labourers, three blacksmiths, a carpenter, a weaver and a tailor. Some of these were exempted from service because of poverty or large families to support, or else where, in the case of two men, the constable has written 'poor' and 'wants the right eye'. The order is signed by one William Blennerhasset, the Chief Constable of the Ward. Three years later, in 1810, the picture is roughly the same, except for the addition of a miller, a joiner and a cabinet maker. An exemption from service is also made for someone who 'wants first finger of right hand'. The missing trigger finger may just have been an accident, but it was also a traditional way of avoiding military service. One can certainly understand why some poorer people might have wanted to get out of militia service. The militia for the whole of Cumberland had to gather once a year in Carlisle to be trained and exercised for 28 days, which would have been disastrous for someone working a small farm, and there was always the threat that the militia might have to turn out and fight. A

BLENNERHASSET AND KIRKLAND.

Barnes, Geo. corn miller.

Fawcett, Thos.

Harrison, Mr. Jno. Kirkland cottage.

Hodgson, Ann, gentlewoman.

Mann, Thos. cartwright.

Palmer, John, schoolmaster.

Routledge, Jph, blacksmith.

Simpson, Jas. shoemaker.

Slater, Mr. Wm., Guards.

Farmers.
*Thus * are Yeomen.*

*Cape, Jph., Guards.

Fell, John. Ferguson, PA.

Hayton, Thos., Guards.

Highmore, Jph., Guards.

Little, Wm., Fitz.

Moore, John, Green.

*Moore, Thos., Overgate.

Temporan, Jph.

Wood, Jph., Guards.

Youdale, John.

The list of inhabitants of Blennerhasset as it appeared in Mannix and Whellan: History, Gazetteer and Directory of Cumberland, 1847. *The list only included the principal inhabitants of the village.*

later list, of 1811, reports someone as having absconded.

The list of occupations is, of course, incomplete, and even more so in the later years of the war, when the age limit for Militia service was reduced to 30, but the picture is, as one would expect, a community of farmworkers together with a number of others serving its needs. A fuller picture emerges from the 1841 census: the occupations are still mainly agricultural, but there also two shoemakers and there is a mention for the first time of a shopkeeper. 'Faith Iredale, grocer'. She is still there, aged 60, in the 1851 census, but by 1861 the business has been taken over by Richard Thompson, 64, still there in 1871. 1851 also shows a blacksmith, a joiner, two tailors, a mason, a number of people living on their own means and, at the other end of the scale, a parish pauper - a poor blind woman supported by the parish. In that year the village had 38 dwellings and 174 inhabitants. There are all kinds of reasons why so many people lived in so few houses. Some families, but not all that many, had large numbers of children, some lived with relatives, some had live-in servants or lodgers. Farm labourers often lived in the farmhouse with the farmer's family

The 1871 census records schoolteachers for the first time Jonathan and Eliza Sharp, teachers at the British School, and two other teachers, though it is not clear whether these two also worked at the British School (for more on this see the section on schools) or perhaps at Torpenhow or Bothel which also had schools. There is also the first record of two seamstresses. Both the number of occupied houses and the number of inhabitants have gone down slightly, but after this low point the population begins to rise quite rapidly and for the first time some actual locations are given: at Blennerhasset Mill, Elizabeth Barnes, a widow, lived with five children and two servants. Blennerhasset Farm, 100 acres, (this must refer to the farm at the east end of the village, although the land taken over by Mechi Farm was also known as Blennerhasset Farm) was jointly worked by William Pattinson and his son, with two farm labourers, while the daughter acted as housekeeper, helped by a domestic servant. Mechi farm (see later for a fuller account), 100

BLENNERHASSET AND KIRKLAND.

Post Money Order Office, and Savings Bank at John Blacklock's, Blennerhasset. Letters via Wigton arrive at 8-30 a.m., and are despatched at 6-30 p.m. No Sunday business.

Parish Council - T. S. Redpath, chairman ; William Blacklock, Jonathan Bland, John Dobie, Thomas Laidlaw, Saul Miller, Joseph Robinson, Thomas T. Robinson, John C. Maxwell. Robert Martin, clerk to the Council.

School Board - W. Blacklock, J. Bland, R. Martin, C. Maxwell.

Allhallows Contributory District - Rev. J. Wordsworth, J. Nixon. Robert Lawson, solicitor, Wigton, clerk to the Board.

Marked 1 reside at Blennerhasset.

1 Blacklock John, grocer and postmaster
1 Blacklock William, estate joiner
1 Board School ; John Stephenson, master ; Miss Bradshaw, assistant
1 Bradshaw Mrs. Mary, dressmaker
1 Brown James, tailor
Cape The Misses Ann and Mary, Orchard house, Kirkland Guards
Cape Messrs. John Henry and Matthew Rayson, Orchard house, Kirkland Guards
Collins Mrs., cowkeeper, Kirkland Guards
1 Graham Michael, check weighman
1 Hanvey William, shoemaker
Ismay James, vict. and farmer, King's Arms, Low Wood Nook
1 Jackson Isaac, clerk
Kendal Robert, cowkeeper, Kirkland Green cottage
1 Mann John, joiner and saw mill
1 Martin Robt., assistant overseer, Beech house
1 Moore Robert, shopkeeper
1 Potts Rev. Joseph, The Manse
1 Redpath Thomas Smith, market gardener, The Gardens
1 Robinson Thomas Tindal, estate joiner
1 Robinson Wm., builder, &c., Garth cottage
1 Shanklin John, tailor
1 Tiffen Mrs. Catherine Wilson Henry, tailor, Whitehead Brow

Farmers.

Cape Joseph (yeoman), Kirkland Guards
Carty Thomas (hind), Kirkland Guards
Hall James William (of Cockermouth), Kirkland Guards
Hall Thomas (hind), Home farm, Whitehall
Highmoor Mrs. Sarah, Kirkland Guards
Littleton Thomas, Fitz farm
Miller Saul, Mechi farm
Mitchinson Isaac, Highwood Nook
1 Pattinson John, Bennerhasset farm and mill
Richardson Matthew, Kirkland Green

The Blennerhasset entry in Bulmer's History and Directory of Cumberland, 1901

The cobbler's shop and the Master's House on either side of the east road in the early twentieth century.

acres, was occupied by the bailiff, George Glasshook, and his wife, together with a son, a daughter and a lodger, but workers on this farm were scattered throughout the village, many of them in cottages built specially to accommodate them. Apart from farm labourers many of whom must have worked at Mechi, we find two steam plough engine drivers, a steam plough labourer, a steam plough water carrier, an agricultural chemist and a gas maker. There are also garden labourers, stone masons and builders who must have spent at least part of their time at the farm. And in this census we also have the first mention of miners, just four so far and one railway worker, a plate layer. The population has now shot up to 280, in 61 dwellings. Most of this expansion must have been due to the Mechi farm scheme, which by this time had been running for nine years, but was to be wound up in the following year.

It is in 1881 that the character of the village has really changed. The Mechi farm experiment may have shaken the village up, but it had still been an agricultural activity. Now we also have the great influx of miners, 52 of them. In addition, the 1880

23

Education Act had established compulsory school attendance for all children under 10, so the school was forced to cope with this at the very time when the population of the village was shooting up. In fact, the idea of compulsory education was loosely interpreted: it was difficult to enforce, and until well into the twentieth century children were regularly withdrawn from school during busy times on the farms. This census also shows a greater variety in occupations. Some provided for the growing population, such as two grocers, one doubling up as a coalminer, the other as a carter, a cordwainer (shoemaker in leather), a laundress, a housepainter, a shoemaker, or cobbler, and a tailor. For the first time, a butcher appears, who was also working as a grocer. Some worked further afield: a railway porter, a road contractor and a river watcher (presumably to protect from poachers). Thomas Mann has now added a small farm of eleven acres to his activities as a joiner, in which he is assisted by one of his sons. Education is provided for by a teacher, a sewing mistress and three pupil teachers.

The next two censuses reveal the first signs of the modern age. Miller Tiffen is an electrician-in-charge probably connected with the pits; it seems unlikely that he would have brought any electricity to Blennerhasset. He also sent his daughter to the Durham Training College for Schoolmistresses. For the first time, too, the village has a post office, in 1891 and, in 1901, a postman, a police constable, and a charwoman - the first and only use of this job description.

The Poor

As well as those who had work there were of course those who had none. The saying, "The poor are always with us," certainly applied to the village. Various laws ensuring that help would be given to the poor had existed since the Middle Ages, but in order to make the system more effective the Poor Law Act of 1601 made parishes responsible for their own poor, so some kind of safety net, which we usually associate with the post-war welfare state, was already in place at the beginning of the seventeenth century. Householders who were made members of the parish meeting, or vestry, were authorised to collect the money needed by levying a rate, based on land values. As people became more liable to move from one parish to another, partly as a result of the Civil Wars (1642-51), the Act of Settlement of 1662 obliged parishes to grant relief only to long-term residents or to those born in the parish.

Above: Torpenhow Church

For Blennerhasset the system was organised from the parish church in Torpenhow. The parish was already divided for administrative purposes into four quarters, of which Blennerhasset and Kirkland were one. (The others were Bewaldeth and Snittlegarth, Torpenhow and Whitrigg and Bothel and Threapland) Responsibility was vested in 'The Sixteen', four for each quarter. There was also a churchwarden and an overseer. Going back to 1688 as an example from the limited records available [4], there were some names which will become familiar later on. Among the four Blennerhasset members of The Sixteen were an Atkinson, a Bouch and a Hodgson. The overseer was another Bouch. In that year nine parish paupers, as they were known, were given relief in sums ranging from £1 14s 8d down to 10s. Paupers varied in number but some names come up year after year, including, from 1688 to 1695, 'Parratt's child', who is then replaced by 'old Parratt' who regularly received £1 6s 0d. The overseers tend to remain the same from year to year and sometimes to be replaced, on death perhaps, by a relative. The position of overseer was a desirable one in that it gave a certain amount of power in the parish.

More help was provided by Richard Bouch, probably the overseer mentioned above, who in 1711 left a field 'to the Poor of Blennerhasset Quarter'.[5] This was Gill Bushes, a three-acre field on the western edge of the quarter. The proceeds were to be given out every second day of November at the Parish Church of Torpenhow. Until 1748 it was let for 18s., a rent which was then raised to 20s. and gradually rose after that. Some names reappeared year after year, like James Fleming, from 1716 to 1756, and Phillis Parkin, from 1716 to 1758. The number of recipients varied, hovering usually around six or eight, but from 1799 to 1801 there was only one, a Jane Atkinson, who got £1 18 0 in each of those years. In one year, though, the distribution was reduced by 10s., which was set aside for clearing the field of whins (thistles, gorse and the like). In 1824 the trustees, including the Reverend John Renton, Vicar of Torpenhow, decided to sell the field to George Dawson (soon to become Lord of the Manor of Blennerhasset) for £120. The trustees felt that the sale would 'better fulfil the benefactor's wishes'. Then in 1848 the payments stopped because of the failure of the Penrith bank where the purchase money was deposited. A generous gesture was made by a Joseph Atkinson of Penrith who gave £150 for the purchase of a field in Bothel 'in trust for the Poor of Blennerhasset Quarter' and another £5 for distribution in the meantime. Twelve people were now in receipt of the money.

The new field was called Thornbank and was let annually for £5. In 1849 the number of recipients rose to fourteen, the money now being given out at Christmas. The names on the list did not always remain there for very long, either through death or departure. Eleanor Osmotherly, who was seventh on the list in 1851, had moved up to first place by 1860. The last entry in the record is for 1881, when ten people benefitted, all receiving ten shillings, including Grace Hanvey and Mary Calvert. There was also Mr Addison's Charity, of which there is no record except that in 1750 it had ordered that at 10 o'clock on the first Sunday of every month nine loaves were to he placed on a special shelf in the church and given to the poor after morning service. At least this would have ensured that they came to church first.

But these charities contributed only a small part of the total given to the poor. The sum raised from the Poor Rate, payable by all landowners, was much greater. The rate varied according to economic conditions between one penny and one shilling in the pound on the value of the land held and was a constant subject of complaint by landowners. The sums raised in this way could be as low as £10 and in one year as high as £130. This was the year 1815-16 when prices slumped after the period of prosperity during the Napoleonic wars. Not all the proceeds went to the poor, however. The Parish returns for the Poor Rate[6] had to be filled in on a printed form by one of the overseers and among the headings were 'Expenses incurred by the Removal of Paupers' (these would be the ones who did not belong to the parish); 'Repairs to County Gates and Bridges'; 'Payments to wives and families of Militia Men' (only one payment seems ever to have been made); 'Fees or Salaries to

Overseers', and a number of other liabilities. In 1821 when the rate was one shilling in the pound the lowest contribution was paid by Thomas Floater, ninepence for his cottage and garden on the north side of the road in the east of the village; the highest by William Hurst, who had to stump up £6 0s 3d.

Landowners, Tenants and Labourers

The farming scene was very different in those days. Now we are accustomed to seeing just a few farms in the area, each of them owned and managed by one farmer. In the eighteenth century and much of the nineteenth, fields were constantly changing hands. Buyers of fields were more like modern property developers and speculators and many of them were not necessarily much concerned about buying fields which would join up to make a proper farm as we know it today. Large farms certainly existed - there were two in Blennerhasset in the early nineteenth century - but North Cumberland was notorious for the number of people who farmed small fields of a few acres and worked their horses, not to speak of themselves, to death, trying to make a living out of them. 'Every man lives upon his own small tenement and the practice of accumulating farms hath not yet made any considerable progress' observe

West Court, also known as Peare Tree Yard, age uncertain. The buildings were originally part of a farm owned at one time by Mr Benson. They are now private dwellings.

two county historians, writing in 1777 [7]. One can assume from this that Cumberland, as so often, was behind the rest of the country in its farming practice.

Agriculture could be a profitable business, not so much for the people who actually worked the land, as for those who owned it, or sold it on for a profit. Hardly any of these landowners lived in the village, and some of them would rarely have come to look at their land once they had bought it. All the same, they are the ones about whom most information is available because their names figure on the deeds, indentures, sales of property and other legal documents. Details of the lives of those who worked the land usually have to be sought for in the few contemporary accounts of life in the area.

Apart from those tenant farmers who had enough land to give themselves a reasonably prosperous lifestyle, most tenants, working their few acres with little help except from members of their own families, were poor. The labourers on the larger farms were even poorer. The same historians say that the cottagers' houses were 'mean beyond imagination'. They ate oaten bread, whereas 'people of condition ate wheat bread', they nearly all wore blue check shirts because blue dye was exempt from duty on printed calicoes, and of course they wore clogs. Usually illiterate and with little power to improve their conditions of work, they lived in what to us is almost inconceivable poverty, and this perhaps partly explains why they tended to move from place to place every few years in the hope of finding something a little better than what they had. The only factor which from time to time enabled them to improve their wages was shortage of labour. Farming suffered from a serious shortage of labour when the growth of manufacturing industry led to farm labourers deserting the land for the higher wages on offer in the towns and the mining areas. Some of the effect of these changes must have been felt in the remote villages of North Cumberland, but Cumberland was always behind the times in reacting to economic developments, the only exception being the coastal areas, where Whitehaven became a prosperous port in the eighteenth century. The one, and possibly only, effect of this prosperity on Blennerhasset was that George Dawson (see the section on Fields and Houses), a wealthy merchant of Whitehaven, was able to buy first land and then the Lordship of the Manor of Blennerhasset in the nineteenth century[8].

After the difficult years of the early 1790s, the end of the eighteenth century and the early years of the nineteenth were good years for landowners, though not necessarily for their tenants and the farm labourers. Thanks to the long-running conflict with France in the Revolutionary and Napoleonic Wars (1793-1815), demand for home-grown produce rose, and so, of course, did food prices and land values. The economic situation for farmers would look a lot less rosy from 1815 onwards, especially in 1816. This was "the year without a summer" when, as a result of a huge volcanic eruption the previous year in distant Tambora, in Indonesia, a cloud of ash reached Europe. With the sun obscured, frosts lasted until June and began again in August, and violent storms caused heavy rainfall and flooding. This must have been one of the few times when Blennerhasset was directly affected by events on the other side of the world. But in the years before the end of the war, every acre of land was highly desirable. And the township of Blennerhasset and Kirkland was, as it still is, mostly farmland. The difference was that there were far more small fields of two or three acres and they all had names.

It s a pity that so many of these picturesque names have now been more or less forgotten. Over to the west of the parish, towards Bothel and Aspatia, there were Burnbutts, Coal Hill, Burtriggs Pasture Field and another Burtriggs. Moving closer to the village, there were Mire Ing (one name which survives), Wains Old Kiln, Wains Fitts, both from the name of a former owner, Broats and several fields called Spear Crooks (or sometimes Sphere Crooks) to the north of the road to Arkleby (now usually known as the back road). To the south of the road lay Wet Flatt, Charlton's, Cudbutts Close and Longlands Cow Mire. Along the High Road towards the main Carlisle-Cockermouth road were Filly Bitts, Boon Banks and Honey Pot. Others, which I have not been able to locate, were Pot

Holes, Bull Coppy and Scurvy Bank. These are only a few of the fields which existed in the early nineteenth century and numbered well over a hundred. There is probably little reason why these names should have survived. Many of the fields, though not all, were absorbed into bigger ones. When Mechi farm (of which more later) was set up in the 1S60s the whole area it covered was reshaped and many of the old fields disappeared with their names for ever. Now that most fields form part of established large farms, there is no particular reason why anyone should want to remember these names.

Land ownership in the past existed in two main forms. Freehold meant roughly what we understand by it today. Owners could do what they liked with the land, let it, sell it or pass it on to their heirs. The only difference was that they paid what was called a free rent to the Chief Lord, or Superior Lord of the Manor, as well as land tax, a heriot and sometimes tithes (explained below). The Chief Lord for this area, higher in status than the Lord of the Manor, was the Earl of Egremont, and the privilege was passed on to later members of the family, the Wyndhams. The other category, 'customary land', was land which was occupied according to the 'custom of the manor'. The custom dated back to medieval times, when the Lord of the Manor (a manor usually occupied the same area as the township) received various services from his tenants in exchange for the land they occupied. As time went on, it became more convenient to receive cash in place of these services. We can get some idea of what these services were from the agreement of 1701 by which one John Jackson, yeoman of Blennerhasset, in return for a payment of £6 0 0. was released from boon services by the then Lord of the Manor, Sir Francis Salkeld, whose home was at Whitehall, a mansion near Blennerhasset[9].

Jackson was no longer subject to 'Boon Services Boon Carriages (then as now legal documents contained no punctuation) and other small dues hereafter mentioned that is to say one day ploughing one day harrowing one day mowing two days shearing one day leading (carting) corn one day leading coals not exceeding eighteen load in the year one carriage with horse to and from Steel End one penny green hew (the right to cut wood or undergrowth on the Lord's estate) and two pence for each swine that is kept upon the premises.'

One can imagine that John Jackson was glad to be relieved of these chores and payments, even if he didn't have to carry out the work himself, but the land he occupied was still 'customary', which meant that a rent had to be paid on it. Moreover, every time the Lord of the Manor changed, and every time the land changed tenants, a fine had to be paid. There is a record of a fine of £10 2 6 received in 1750 from Sir Alfrid Lawson by Margaret Salkeld on the death of Henry Salkeld Esq 'my Late Husband the last general Admitting Lord of Blennerhasset and Upmanby'. Two years later Sir Alfrid died and his heir Sir Wilfrid Lawson had to pay another fine[10].

These changes in ownership were formally recorded at the manorial court, which might be held in the lord's house, if he lived near enough, but this was not always the case. William Charlton, who was Lord of the Manor in the late eighteenth and early nineteenth centuries, lived at Hesleyside, near Newcastle. He had inherited the Manor from his aunt, Margaret Salkeld of Whitehall. In such cases the Court might be held at the local inn. There was a set formula for these transactions. Here is the record of the transfer of a property in 1787 from Joseph Atkinson to his brother-in-law Anthony Harrison. a surgeon living in Penrith.[11]

'Be it remembered that on the Twenty third Day of March in the Year of our Lord 1787 Came Anthony Harrison Surgeon and took of the Lord of the said Manor Before Thomas Benson Gentleman Steward of the said Manor upon the Surrender of Joseph Atkinson One Tenement with the Appurtenance in Blennerhasset of the yearly Customary Rent of Thirteen Shillings To Hold the same unto the said Anthony Harrison during the Joint Lives of the Lord and Tenant according to the custom of the said Manor.' Unfortunately these documents don't indicate the whereabouts of the property.

The fines and the yearly rent were not all, though. There was the heriot, which originated in medieval times as a handover of weapons, horses and other military equipment to a Lord on the death of his tenant. Then the payment came to be that of the best live beast or dead chattel and by the eighteenth century the payment was made in cash, based on the value of the best beast. In I 752, as well as the fine noted above, Sir Wilfrid Lawson was charged £16 16 0 'being the value of a Horse taken for a Heriot due to me as Lady of the Manor of Blennerhasset and Upmanby'[12]. The smallest recorded heriot paid around this time was 6d. This was required of Martha Peile of Holm Cultram in 1757. She had bought for £50 a freehold house and land from Joseph Greenup, a weaver from Setmurthy. She died in 1793 but the property was still known as Peile's Croft until the 1860s, when the Congregational Church built its new Manse on the ruins of the old house. As the land was freehold, not customary, she paid a rent of one peppercorn to 'the Lady of White Hall (this was Margaret Salkeld) if demanded also Six pence a year for a hen (this, it seems, was her best beast) and no other taxes whatsoever either Parliamentary or Parochial'[13]. A peppercorn was traditionally paid when no rent was required. Something, however small, and a peppercorn certainly qualified as small, had to be paid, or else the transaction would not have been valid. The parliamentary tax mentioned was the Land Tax. Everyone had had to pay it since the 1690s when it was introduced by Parliament to pay for a war (one of many) against France. Presumably Martha Peile was not required to pay it on such a small property: it would have been included in the tax paid by Margaret Salkeld.

A further tax for which some properties were liable was the tithe. This was originally a tenth of the value of the produce and payable to the church, but since the Reformation many of these tithes had been transferred from the church to laymen (known as 'lay impropriators'). while others had been dropped completely in return for a suitable payment. Many Blennerhasset properties were now tithe-free. Further dues are mentioned in a handwritten sale bill of 1786. These were payable on a nine-acre property on the north side of the township

'To be sold in Publick Sale on Wednesday 31st day of May 1786 All that freehold and Tythe Free Close of Arable and Meadow Ground called Ellen Bridge situate lying and being within the Township of Blennerhasset - Subject to the payment of one farthing, half farthing to the purvey rate, four pence three farthings to Cornish rent and three farthings to Dashwood rent.' (To any readers unfamiliar with the old currency, a farthing was a quarter of an old penny, 12 pence made a shilling and twenty shillings a pound, so there were 240 pence in a pound - and 960 farthings!)

The survey was a national tax to meet general expenses and a certain sum was fixed against each parish and then divided up amongst the properties. It was abolished by Act of Parliament in 1810 because it was found to be unfair in operation. 'Cornish rent' should actually be spelt 'cornage' and was originally a form of rent based on the number of horned cattle; it was another term for the free rent mentioned above, and payable to the Chief Lord. Dashwood rent is something of a mystery.[14] Inquiries made to the local archives, the local history department of Lancaster University and the Oxford English Dictionary have drawn a blank. It was also called 'Sheriff Aid' and was payable on all property, perhaps to finance the constabulary. The mystery is only deepened by a later document stating that it was payable to a Margaret Bennett, daughter of the late Joseph Sanderson of Maryport for rents from Michaelmas 1799 to Michaelmas 1827 at 6s a year totalling £8 8 0 for 28 years. It seems that someone had woken up to the fact that it hadn't been paid for a long time. A note at the end says: 'It would be much better if the township of Blennerhasset would purchase them at 20 years purchase'. This may have been done, as Dashwood rents seem to have disappeared from the records early in the nineteenth century.

Another tax which all landowners were required to pay was the `Lord's Rent', a sum based on the property valuation and payable annually to the Lord of the Manor. There are records of the payments to Sir Wilfrid Lawson from 1868 until 1895, when the system seems to have been abandoned. This was probably because of the increasing reluctance of landowners to pay it. Sometimes the rent was not paid for several years and in some cases not at all. In 1879 the entry for J.Pattinson of Blennerhasset mill, who was due to make two payments of 13s 6d, is marked 'refused to pay'. 13s 6d was in fact quite a large sum; most payments were under 2s and in a few cases only 1d.

In 1797. instructions were given to Mr Mounsey, Steward of the Lord of the Manor, (there is still a Mounsey's Solicitors in Carlisle today) to prepare 'enfranchisements' for 14 customary properties, which meant that these customary owners had the chance to become freeholders.[15] The occupiers of the properties had to pay their heriots and also 'for our respective customary rents twenty five years purchase'. And so, to have the freehold of their property, the owners had a considerable sum to pay, but one which would begin to pay off after twenty five years had elapsed. They all seemed to think it worthwhile except for Thomas Benson, who preferred his land to remain customary[16] and thus it remained, with his eldest son and customary heir, the Reverend John Benson, paying a fine of £113 when his father died in 1807, and so with all the succeeding Bensons. until the estate was sold for £4,050 to Sir Wilfrid Lawson in 1860 and then became incorporated in Mechi Farm[17]. After Thomas, the Bensons could have had very little interest in the land, except as a money-earner, since they were dispersed around the country, most of them joining the clergy. One of them, the Reverend Christopher Benson (1788-1868) the last owner, is the only one of the Blennerhasset landowners, apart from Sir Wilfrid Lawson, distinguished enough to have achieved a mention in the *Dictionary of National Biography*. The Blennerhasset properties formed only a small part of the Benson estates; they also included land in Bolton, Brigham, Cockermouth, Embleton, Greysouthen, Allhallows and as far away as Egremont and Cleator.

Fields, Farms and Houses

Towards the end of September 1798 an important sale was held in Blennerhasset[18]. Jane Atkinson, nee Harrison, was selling the properties of her husband, Joseph, who had died, aged 44, in 1790. There were eight lots, varying in size from 16 acres to just over one acre. The estate had in fact gone bankrupt. The *Cumberland Pacquet* of 6 June, 1797, announces the assignment of the estate to trustees, including Hodgson the Elder and Hodgson the Younger, who were themselves, as we shall see, important landowners in the village. Joseph Atkinson was a yeoman, a title which meant that he farmed a fairly large property and had therefore been a person of some standing. Most of the inhabitants of Blennerhasset who worked the land, and most of them did, were tenant farmers, or else labourers working for them. One of the sale notices (see illustration) has fortunately been preserved and was the one used by Thomas Benson. who bought lots 3, 4, and 5 and took a share in lots 7 and 8. One can see from the sums written on the sale notice, not to speak of the

Above: Present day Peare Tree Cottage.

Estate at Blennerhassett.

TO BE SOLD,
IN PUBLIC,
UPON THE PREMISES,

On Thursday the 27th of September, 1798,
AT SIX O'CLOCK IN THE EVENING,
(TOGETHER OR IN PARCELS,)

A

Freehold Messuage & Tenement,

SITUATE AT BLENNERHASSETT,

In the Parish of Torpenhow, in Cumberland,

Late the Estate of Mr. Joseph Atkinson, deceased;

Consisting of

Handwritten margin note: "Total outgoings 5/2 Dashwood"

	A.	R.	P.
A Dwelling House, Barn, Byar, Stable and other Out-houses, Garden and Orchard and three Closes, called—the Croft, the Nook and Highlands, now in the Possession of Mrs. Jane Atkinson, containing together	6	1	2
Four Closes, called—High Weskhouse, Low Weskhouse, Heads Meadow and Folly Close, in the Possession of Cuthbert Raper, Edward Bell and Mrs. Atkinson, containing together about	9	0	14
Two Closes, called—Sphere Crooks, in the Possession of Mrs. Atkinson, containing together	3	0	6
Near Pasture Close, in the Possession of Joseph Calvert, containing	4	2	30
Four Closes, called—Far Pasture, Burtrigg, Burtrigg Meadow and Gill Heads Meadow, in the Possession of William Gunson, Joseph Jackson and William Jackson, containing together	16	3	20
Two Closes, called—Hard Meadow and Crofts, in the Possession of John Jackson and George Black, containing together	4	3	5
A Close, called—Cow Mire, in the Possession of James Scott, containing	2	0	15
A Close, called—Wilson's Meadow, in the Possession of James Scott, containing	1	3	10
	48	2	19

Handwritten figures in margins: 261·0 · 3, 265, 110, 100, 335, 120, 10, 23 / 1224·, 545, 679- ; 24.2.1 ; 2 0., 26 2 ; 27-10-0, 545—0·0., 76/24

The Whole of the above Estate is well watered and fenced, is near to Coal and Lime, and has a valuable Right of Common of Pasture and Turbary upon Aspatria Common.

A Deposit of Ten per Cent. on the Purchase-Money, to be paid at the Time of Sale, and the Residue at Candlemas next, when the Purchaser shall enter upon the Premises.

For further Particulars apply to Mrs. Jane Atkinson, of Blennerhassett, (who will shew the Premises,)—or to Mr. Harrison, Attorney at Law, Penrith.

Opposite; The sale notice used by Thomas Benson, who bought lots 3, 4, and 5 and took a share in lots 7 and 8. One can see from the sums written on the sale notice, not to speak of the complicated calculations (additions, subtractions and long divisions) with which he covered the other side of the page, (above) that Thomas Benson's main concern was with how much he would be liable for, and how much he was likely to gain.

complicated calculations (additions, subtractions and long divisions) with which he covered the other side of the page, that Thomas Benson's main concern was with how much he would be liable for, and how much he was likely to gain. Already a landowner, as we have seen, he and his descendants would for some time to come be amongst the biggest landowners in the village. He was also Steward of the Lord of the Manor as mentioned in the quotation above from the Court record of 1787. The *Cumberland Pacquet* of 1775 describes him as 'an eminent attorney of Cockermouth' and also reports in the same year that 'a genteel new home now building' near Carlisle, belonging to him, had been broken into and vandalised.

The sale notice needs a little explanation. A messuage was a dwelling house its outhouses and the surrounding land. A tenement could mean any permanent property or real estate, in this case the various fields for sale. The 'Byar' mentioned in Lot 1 is a cowhouse Possession means occupancy and refers to the tenants of the land. The right of turbary on Aspatria Common was the right to dig for turf or peat. Candlemas (2 February) was one of the Quarter Days when payments were traditionally due. It was, in fact, a Scottish quarter day, the English and Welsh having a different system.

The main body of land he bought, totalling just over 24 acres, lay to the east of the village. 24 acres may not sound much in modern farming terms, but the fact that he paid £625 for it, a sizeable sum in those days, shows how profitable land ownership could be. Thomas Benson had already established himself as a landowner in the parish by buying the estate of Robert Martindale[19]. Not much is known about Martindale and not much was known during his lifetime either. He had owned fields in various scattered parts of the parish and, according to a note written in a schedule of property drawn up some years later in 1808: 'On the 1st of January 1783 Robert Martmdale mortgaged the above estate to Mr Benson for one hundred pounds. Mr Benson only now stands Tenant and Mortgagee. Query - if Mr Martindale is living or dead who is his heir at law?' The question was never answered, it seems, but there are some further details about Martindale's problems. He was running into debt and the sums he borrowed show how desperate the situation was getting. He began by borrowing £300, then £50, £60 and £40, followed by a number of smaller sums totalling £40.6.11 and finally £2.3 1. In 1787 he borrowed another £74 from Benson, bringing his total debt up to £670, and would soon need more. The result was that his property, being 'scant security' for the loans, went up for sale in 1788 and most of it seems to have gone to Benson. That, together with the land bought from Joseph Atkinson, stayed, as we have seen, with the Bensons. As for Robert Martindale, the

40

mortgage to Benson was still not settled. A note made on the mortgage by the solicitor in 1794, reads: 'It appears he has defaulted' and doubts were still being expressed in 1812 about whether he still had any rights over the land. But the man himself seems to have disappeared for ever.

While the Benson lands stayed with them for seventy years or so, the other properties in the Joseph Atkinson sale were to know a variety of owners. A group of fields to the north of the western end of the village on either side of the river Ellen, the Croft, the Nook and Wilson's Meadow on the south side of the river and Highlands, also called Overwaters, on the north side, and which figured as lots 1 and 8 in the Joseph Atkinson sale, were sold in 1799 by William Grave, who would now become the tenant, to Sir Wilfrid Lawson of Brayton Hall[20]. The purchase included a house, barn and garden on the north side of the Township of Blennerhasset. Sir Wilfrid's outgoings were listed as follows:

'The yearly free rent of Six Pence called Cornage to the Earl of Egremont the Chief Lord of the Fee thereof Five Pence half penny Dashwood rent One half penny to each Purvey and One Shilling and Six Pence three farthings the proportion for the said Premises to the sum Seven Shillings the Land Tax for the whole of the said Joseph Atkinson's Tenements at Blennerhasset and to repair Nine yards in length of the Road from Brayton to Bagrow [sic] '

Only four years later Sir Wilfrid exchanged this land 'for mutual convenience' with John Hodgson senior and John Hodgson junior, also considerable landowners, for some land lying slightly to the east[21]. As was so often the case with these transactions, the deal came with conditions: the Hodgsons had to 'wall, fence or hedge each of the sides of the four closes and repair same, along the Ellen, and set up a new water rail across the Ellen to prevent any escape of livestock up, down or across the river'. Sir William's commitment was lighter: he simply had to put up a wall, fence or hedge where a tiny piece of land called the Corner bordered the river (on its north side) and set up a water rail there.

Of the remaining lots in the Atkinson sale, lot 2 went to John

Tawson
6. 0. 31 44 v
Over Waters
Hodgsons 4 2.0
and part of
Atkinsons 3

Over Wate
and Canal

former
Jos Atkin
50 v

From Sir W
Tawson to
Hodgson
Garden & Or
Croft, Nook
and Wilsons
Meadow
4. 0. 10

4. 3. 29

52 v

Hodgson
Croft
8. 3. 15

47 v

Hodgson
2. 0. 0 &
Atkinsons
Croft

Old Kiln
Benson
Custmry
1. 1. 36

46 v

Wains
Old
Kiln
2. 2. 36
from Wain
& Hodgson

Plantation
0. 0. 6 49 v
from Hodgson
& Atkinson old Kiln

Wheat Close
1. 1. 31
from Charlton

48 v

53 v

Wai
61 v

BLEN

15

Dawsons
Cottage

Dawson
from
Charlton
Croft & Garten

0. 3. 3
55 Dawson
from
Peele
Mill Croft

169 v

Charltons Croft
13. 0. 4

From Charlton

Wheat Close
Croft

Meadow from Charlton

174 v

0. 2. 4
Charltons
back
Close
Hays
parcel

1799
Werk House
w Do.
s Meadow
Close
3. 17
Atkinson

0. 3. 34

Gongland
1. 3. 26 2 f
from Ha
one field or

Meadow
38

1. 6

Bl
Lion
C

1. 2. 10
Plan

42

Adjoing sections of a late nineteenth century tracing of an early nine-teeth century map made for Sir Wilfrid Lawson. The names on the fields refer to the owners prior to Sir Wilfrid.

Buildings at one side of West Court, used by the farm and now for storage. The yellow-painted section (light colour, bottom right) once housed four lavatories for the use of the inhabitants.

White. This consisted of four adjacent fields to the south of the village, High and Low Weskhouse (or Weskas), Heads Meadow and Folly Close which he made into one ten-acre field. It was sold by John White's son Joseph to John Dawson in 1854. It then went to Sir Wilfrid Lawson in 1860 and shortly afterwards was swallowed up in the Mechi Farm Estate

The Benson lands were scattered all over the parish, from the western edge to the High Road and from the River Ellen to the southern border. Only one building was included, which stood in the area now known as Pear Tree Yard or West Court.. These fields must have been considered something of a nuisance by other landowners, for as the nineteenth century progressed more effort was made to buy adjacent fields which would make up a proper farm, either by purchasing any land which came up for sale or by exchanges, like the one between Sir Wilfrid Lawson and John Hodgson. By the middle of the nineteenth century the chief landowners were the Hodgson descendants and the Dawsons, the latter being also Lords

44

of the Manor. Hodgson and Dawson were 'statesmen' (more properly 'estatesmen'), farming their own fairly large farms and having the title 'gentleman'.

George Dawson, described as a merchant, and living in Whitehaven, became Lord of the Manor of Blennerhasset and Upmanby in 1830, having purchased it, together with the 160 acres of land attached to the Manor (the 'demesne lands'), for £587 2 0[22]. This shows what a dramatic fall there had been in land prices since 1798, when Thomas Benson paid £625 for a mere 24 acres. The sellers were the heirs of William Charlton of Hesleyside. George Dawson was a very wealthy man. In his will of 1832 he bequeaths to his nephew John Dawson his Blennerhasset and Bothel estate, the Manor of Blennerhasset, land in the nearby parishes of Bromfield and Allhallows, warehouses in Antigua, ships' shares and financial securities.

George Dawson seems to have been very cautious about his purchases. When he bought the Hodgson land resulting from the insolvency of the Hodgson son (see below) he received the bill for £11,614 from the solicitors in 1817, but in 1819 he had still signed nothing[23]. A letter between the two solicitors concerned enquires why he is asking for documents he has already seen and insists that there is no mortgage on the property. A further letter says, 'Mr Dawson's speedy Determination relating to the same will be expected'. The determination, speedy or not, must eventually have been received, and Dawson became a major landowner of the village.

George Dawson died in 1842 and his nephew John entered into his inheritance, now enlarged by the purchase of the Hodgson land as well as various other small properties. A plan of the Dawson estate, made at some time during the 1850s, shows its extent, covering most of the land south of the Ellen and west of the village and also revealing what inconvenience must have been caused by the scattered Benson lands which intrude like wedges at various points on the plan[24]. John was anxious to improve the farm. In 1846 he began building a 'thrashing machine'[25]. This was not in itself an

CONTENTS

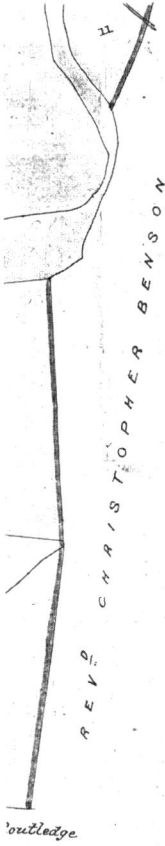

N°		A	R	P
1	Houses, Yards &c	.	3	15
2	Croft	4	1	19
3	Plantation	.	.	33
4	Wheat Close	1	1	28
5	Wains Old Kiln	2	2	32
6	Mire Ing	6	.	28
7	Wains Fills	11	2	22
8	Whitrigg Heads	1	0	31
9	Charleton's Garth	1	.	.
10	Peile's Croft	.	3	10
11	Charleton's Back Close	1	.	36
12	Lane	.	2	12
13	Charleton's Croft	13	.	12
14	Longland's Meadow	2	2	10
15	Longland's	13	2	24
16	Longland's Sike	7	3	19
17	Longland's Cow Mire	3	1	6
18	Wains little Heads Close	2	3	26
19	Charleton's Cudbutts Close	5	3	14
20	Wains far Head Close	3	3	14
21	Charleton's East Heads	11	2	38
22	Watering Place	.	1	36
23	Charleton's West Heads	14	1	14
24	New Close	4	.	39
25	D°	4	.	26
26	Wet Flatt	11	2	4
27	Pasture Field	8	1	10
28	Fell Burtrigg Head	4	2	36
29	Burtrigg's Meadow	6	1	30
30	Charleton's Burtrigg	13	1	14
31	West Burtrigg	14	3	12
32	Burtrigg End	3	2	36
33	Burnibutts	9	3	16
34	Coal Hill	14	2	.7
35	Gill Heads	7	3	20
36	Gill Bushes	3	0	28
37	Coal Hole Close	4	1	38
38	Bothel Park	19	1	34
39/40	Burtrigg's Pasture field	7	0	36
41/42	Weskhouse otherwise Weskans	10	2	27
	Total	260	1	12

A list of the fields owned by Mr Dawson with their areas in acres, rods and perches.

46

The sluice gate in the bank of the river. The ratchet mechanism for raising it is in the bottom centre of the picture.

innovative project. William Dickinson, writing in 1853, says that the machine 'is become very general over all the grain-growing parts of the county'[26]. The figure for 1849 (presumably including Dawson's machine) was 306, 71 of which were driven by water (reckoned to be the best method), 7 by steam, one by wind and the rest by horses. Dawson's was water-driven. In 1846 he was granted the right to cut a mill-race from the River Ellen, on the east side of Ann Hodgson's property (The Croft), 'The land to be covered with soil so that the land can be used again'. The mill race was later used for the sawmill (now converted into a private house) at the western end of the village and then extended to Mechi Farm. The sluice gate can still be seen in the bank of the river together with the mechanism for raising it. Not so long ago children used to run through the mill-race if the water was not too high, entering at the river and coming out at the sawmill.

The builder's account booklet has survived, showing the daily rate he earned. This varies between 2s 6d and 3s 0d, a fair wage for the time. We also have the subsistence expenses for the men 'rearing timber' 'Bread - 5s 0d, Beef- 13s 0d, Whiskey - 13s 6d, Rum - 7s 0d,

47

Ale - 12s 0d'. One can understand why the Temperance movement was pursued with such enthusiasm, notably by Sir Wilfrid Lawson. The materials used were 'leading tiles, soil, nails, cement, railings, hair, laths, 200 bricks, Lazonby flags' and the total cost came to £618 9 5½ This was an exceptionally expensive machine, and Dawson was already overstretched, since in the same year, 1846, he had taken out a mortgage for £8,000 on various properties, including Peile's Croft[27]. This did not stop him buying more land (see the paragraphs on the Joseph Atkinson estate) in 1854. He then mortgaged the whole of the Blennerhasset and Bothel estate as security for a £25,000 'running account' and then, his final defeat, he mortgaged the Manor itself to the Bank of Whitehaven. The bank informed him of its intention to sell the estate in 1860 if he did not pay off the mortgage. There was no hope of his doing that, and later in the same year the whole property, plus the Manor, was put up for sale at the Globe Hotel (still there) in Cockermouth, and bought by Sir Wilfrid Lawson for £17,100.

The story of the Hodgson estate is rather different, although it too eventually ended in the hands of Sir Wilfrid. There were in fact three John Hodgsons. Hodgson senior was born in 1733 and died, aged 88, in 1821[28]. His son died some time before 1805 and his grandson, known as Hodgson junior, or sometimes Hodgson the younger, was born in 1790 and died, aged 32, the year after his grandfather. The Hodgsons, at the turn of the century, owned a large part of the land in the village, but suffered a terrible setback when the son (the middle one) died insolvent with debts of £18,000. The fact that in 1788 he had married Miss Fletcher, 'an amiable young lady, with a fortune of £4,000', as *The Cumberland Pacquet* reports, could not have helped very much with debts of that size. There is no evidence to say how these colossal debts were accumulated, whether through incompetent management, riotous living, heavy gambling (very popular at the time), sheer bad luck, or a combination of them all. Not surprisingly, it was a long time before the matter was settled. It was only in 1816 that John the younger released the 250-acre estate in Bothel and Blennerhasset in trust to his father's creditors.

The village playing fields with the cricket pavilion now occupy part of the area once known as Hodgson's Croft.

The 54 creditors are listed and among them are many inhabitants of Blennerhasset, including a John Pingney, to whom the largest single sum, £946 0 10, was owing. Ten of the creditors were illiterate and signed with a cross. The following year the whole estate was sold to George Dawson for £11,614[29]. No evidence is available to show whether the outstanding debt was covered. But this disaster did not mark the end of the Hodgson interest in the village. The descendants of John senior, thanks largely to his efforts, still retained a large number of fields between the north side of the Arkleby road and the river, as well as some to the west of the parish.

By his will, John Hodgson, senior, left all his property to his grandson, who then left it to his wife, Ann[30]. In 1827 she let the land on a nine-year lease at £110 per annum to Isaac Clarke of Blindcrake, keeping apart 'the Little Meadow adjoining the River Ellen' for herself (this is the land across which John Dawson was later to dig his mill race) and some of the houses to the north of the village green, extending northwards to the bend in the river, also known at the time as Hodgson's Croft. Much of this land is now occupied by a playing field. A lease of this length was unusual in this

Tithe-free Estate

AT BLENNERHASSET.

TO BE LET,

BY PROPOSAL, IN WRITING,

And entered upon at Candlemas next,

ALL THAT TITHE-FREE

FARM,

With a good Dwelling-house, Barn, Byer, and Stable, in excellent Repair,

SITUATE AT BLENNERHASSET,

In the Parish of Torpenhow, in the County of Cumberland;

Containing 67 Acres, more or less,

Of good Arable, Meadow, and Pasture Land, now in the Occupation of ISAAC CLARKE, as Tenant.

☞ Mrs. HODGSON of Blennerhasset, will send a Person to shew the Farm; and Proposals will be received by Mr. HEWSON, Conveyancer, Wigton, until the 29th Day of SEPTEMBER ensuing, after which the Tenant will be declared.

AUGUST 15th, 1836.

THOMAS BAILEY, PRINTER, COCKERMOUTH.

The poster for the lease of Mrs Hodgson's farm in 1836. Isaac Clarke was the outgoing tenant

50

part of Cumberland, and strict conditions (a 'husbandry clause') were attached to it. It is worth quoting from them because they give an idea of the way in which farming was practised in Cumberland in the early nineteenth century[31].

Isaac Clarke 'shall at his Costs and Charges well and sufficiently amend glaze and keep in repair all the Glass windows Doors and Locks hedge ditch cast (to clear ditches) cleanse all the Hedges Ditches Quicksets (young hedges made from cuttings) Gates Gate posts and Fences shall not sell exchange or give away any Grass Hay Straw Fodder Corn unthreshed Soil Compost Ashes Manure Muck or Dung that shall grow be made or arise', All this was to be used on the premises 'in a husbandlike manner' 'Horses Mares Horned Cattle and other Cattle' were to be 'bound up in Byer Sheds and Stables for the better increase and making of Dung' Furthermore, any dung, muck, etc., after the last barley harvest was to be kept for Ann Hodgson. Every year half the arable land was to lie fallow or to grass and no more than two crops in succession of wheat, rye, barley, oats, peas, beans or other grain were to be sown. During the last three years of the tenancy, land laid to grass or fallow was to be sown with clover and ryegrass, with not less than 7lb. of red clover seeds and 3lb. of white per acre.

This was 'ley farming', and probably good practice for the time. At the beginning of the century agriculture in Cumberland had been in a poor state and leases, where entered into, had rarely been agreed for more than a few years, so that tenants had little incentive to improve the land. Ann Hodgson had therefore taken good advice in granting a nine-year lease. Even so, leases of up to twenty-one years were routine in other parts of the country. When Isaac Clarke's lease was up she advertised the land again (see illustration). The ownership of the land passed to John and Ann's two daughters, Mary Jane and Ann. Ann died and Mary Jane married a shipbroker, Cornelius Robson from Liverpool, who sold it to Sir Wilfrid in 1865.

One development which is unrecorded in the history of land ownership in Blennerhasset is an Enclosure Act. Enclosures had been taking place in the country since the seventeenth century and

51

Beech Tree Yard, on the north side of the Green. These houses were already shown on an early nineteenth-century map.

became more and more widespread in the eighteenth until the practice was made official by a series of Acts of Parliament (one for each township) in the early nineteenth century. Acts were passed for other townships in the parish (Torpenhow, Bewaldeth and Bothel) but there seems to be no record of one for Blennerhasset. Enclosures replaced the old system of open field farming. Farmers had owned small areas of land but had tended to graze their animals on common land, but new methods of farming which enabled farmers to keep their stock alive over the winter and reduce disease, with the possibility of breeding better animals, made the open field system a liability. Common land was therefore enclosed and distributed among the various users who were considered to have rights over it. It may be that the farmland in Blennerhasset was already well enough distributed for enclosures to be thought unnecessary, but farmers would still have lost their rights to use the common land at Aspatria.

The Bensons, Dawsons and Hodgsons were not the only

The Winder Cottages. On the door lintel are the initials WBM and the text "Feare God" together with the date 1678.
The bottom picture shows the drip-stone that runs the length of the cottage above the windows.

landowners in the township, but they did have the lion's share of it. A plan of the area, originally made in the early nineteenth century and retraced towards the end of the century, probably for Sir Wilfrid Lawson, who had bought most of the land by then to add to the thousands of acres he owned elsewhere in the county, gives the names of the successive owners of most of the fields. Most of these names need not interest us, but if one looks at the past owners of the houses and adjacent land in the village itself, there is one name which still has echoes today. It is Winder, a name which is still remembered on some property in the east of Blennerhasset. In fact the Winders, in the early nineteenth century, lived in the neigh-bouring village of Baggrow. Joseph was a yeoman and landowner, and had farming interests in both villages; his brother William, a joiner and cabinet maker, was the more ambitious one and bought up various properties in both villages, including houses and adjacent fields 'on the south side of the street of the village of Blennerhasset'. These are the properties which still bear the name of Winder, over a century after the Winders had had anything to do with them.

Both Joseph and William bequeathed their possessions to William's son, also William, who died only eight years after his father, in 1852[32]. By this time, the Winders had moved away from the area. As so often happened when a family acquired a certain amount of wealth, the children, benefiting from a better education, moved away to seek their fortunes elsewhere. William, in fact, became a wine and spirit merchant in Newcastle. His two sons were even more adventurous. One went to be a farmer in South America and the other to Australia. The daughter, Mary Jane, stayed in England and administered the property until it was all sold in 1875 to the Reverend William Gunson, who already owned property in Baggrow inherited from his father. William Gunson was a Fellow of Christ's College, Cambridge, another case of a son going off to make good elsewhere. The property then passed to the Creighton family and Harold Creighton (another absentee, living in Devon) sold it to Sir Wilfrid Lawson in 1919[33].

The ages of the older houses in the village are difficult to fix

The well-stocked village shop as it appeared in the early years of the twentieth century.

with any confidence. Certainly many of the houses along the south of the road on the eastern side of the village date back at least to the seventeenth century, like the Winder terrace. There is also one house of the same period on the opposite side of the main road through the village. Many of Blennerhasset's oldest houses fell into ruin and were replaced by newer buildings. This is certainly true of most of the dwellings on the western side of the road. Ruin also seems to have threatened some of those on the east road, but they were rescued in quite recent years. A passage in Kenneth Smith's *Cumbrian Villages* refers to 'a row of dilapidated seventeenth-century cottages next to the old chapel', this would have included the Winder terrace[34]. Probably the ordinary labourers lived, up to the eighteenth century at least, in cottages which would not have been worth restoring. Nicolson and Burn, the county historians, writing in 1777, describe Cumberland cottagers' houses as 'mean beyond imagination, made of mud and thatched with turf'[35].

In summing up the way the village has changed over the last two hundred years, the first available evidence comes from the map

An aerial view of the Village Green taken in 1995. The council houses are to the middle right of the picture.

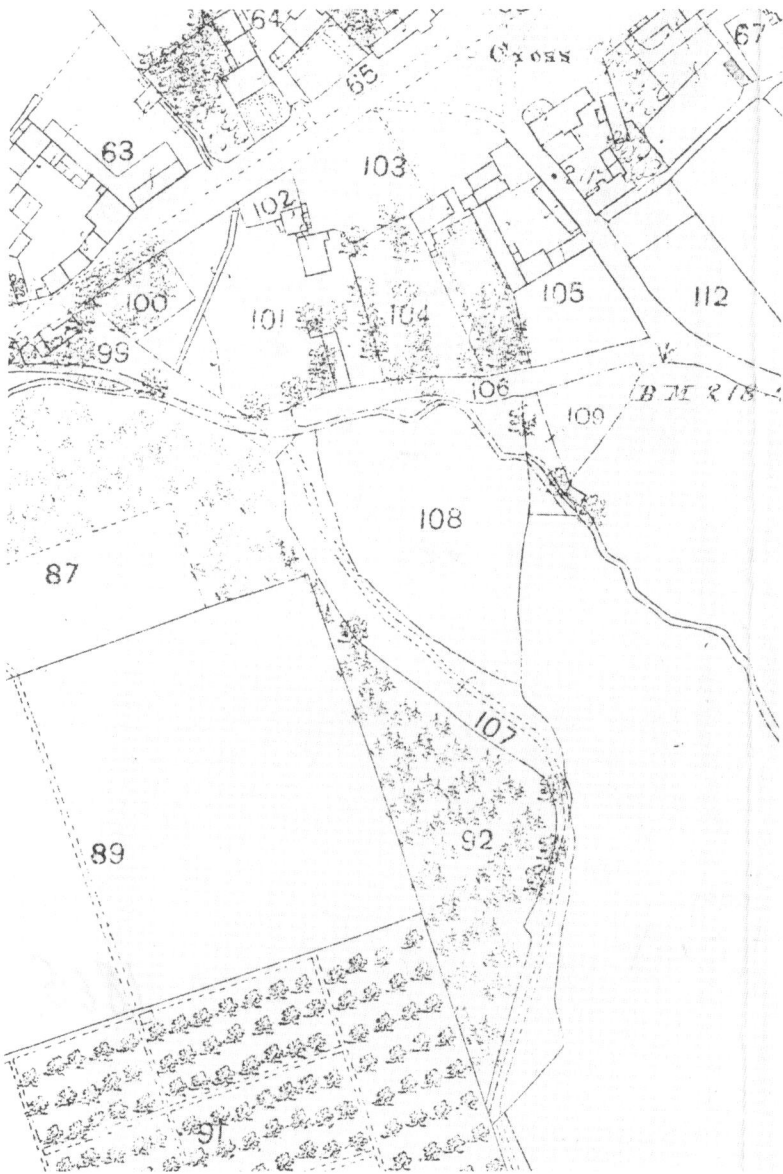

The OS map of 1865 showing the same area.

57

An aerial view from 1995 showing the bridge and the east end of the village. the back of the Shop is to the centre right of the picture.

Gillmour House, which, until 1964, had served as the Manse. It was built in 1864 and the adjoining houses were built a few years later.

I mentioned earlier, dating from the early nineteenth century and retraced for Sir Wilfrid Lawson towards the end of the century.

Looking at the east side of the village, the south side of the street is roughly as it is now including the freestanding cobbler's shop. Here many of the houses go back to at least the seventeenth century: the last one to be built, now known as Brook Cottage, was built in 1763.

On the north side of the street, however, there was only one house, Floater's Cottage. This is perhaps where the largest house on that side of the road now stands, built in 1790. Further to the east is East Farm, a large and solidly built establishment which may be older than any buildings now surviving.

On the west side and south of the green, West Court is there, by the High Road, and on the corner, Peare Tree House, going back to 1686. This is one of the oldest surviving houses on this side of the village. A little to the west, still on the south of the green, was the

59

The old cobbler's shop awaiting a new owner and a new use.

house which originally belonged to Martha Peile, on the land known at that time as Peile's Croft and covering what is now the Manse and Manse Row. At right angles to it, was a whole row of buildings stretching from the road to the back lonning.

The north side of the green was much as it is today, except that there was a smithy by the river and of course no school. The River Ellen follows a slightly different course and no island is shown at the bend in the river.

1865 was the date of the first Ordnance Survey map of the area. There is now a terrace of houses on the north side of the east road a little to the east of the school, which is much smaller in its original form than it is now. On the west side the new Manse has now been built, but there are still no houses between it and the row of houses at the western end of the green, some of which have disappeared. On the Green itself the map marks a cross in the Gothic script used for ancient monuments. This is where the war memorial was later erected. Perhaps it was given the form of a cross in

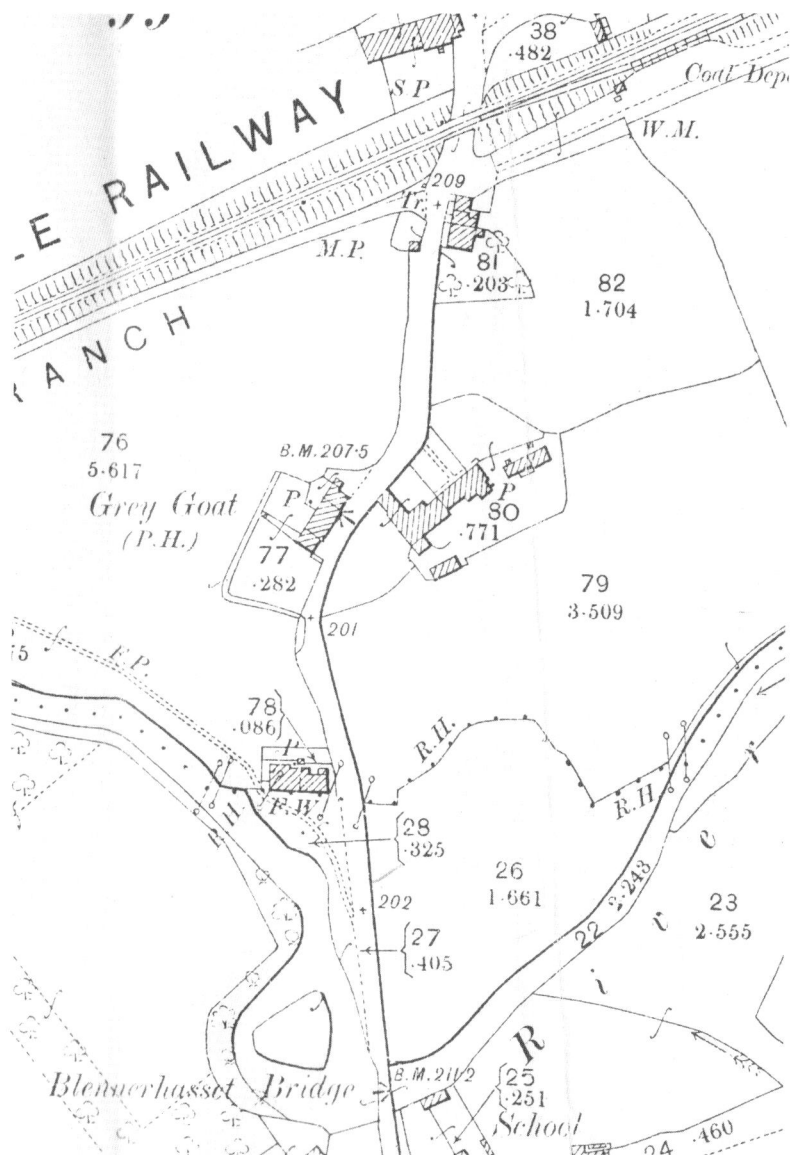

The 1865 OS map showing the course of the River Ellen with the island below the bridge and The Grey Goat in the centre.

recognition of the earlier cross. One can still see an old stone base under the memorial.

Further to the west the biggest development for a long time has taken place, and that is the construction of Mechi Farm, soon to have a mill race extending from where the sawmill now stands. The north side of the Green was much as it is today as far as Beech Tree Yard, but beyond that there is a very different arrangement of buildings and no sawmill is marked. There is also a building on the opposite side of the road, just where the back lonning joins it. The river now has three small islands in it, as it does on a small map drawn up for the Winder property in 1876.

On the next map, which was published in 1900, (the islands have merged into one, and this has got progressively smaller and today sometimes threatens to disappear altogether.) The north side of the east street has more houses and the school dating from the 1850s. has been enlarged. Two cottages, known as Garth Cottages, have been built on the High Road south of West Court and another a bit further down on the other side of the road. Here there is also a pump. On the west side, four terraced cottages have been built onto the Manse and there remains only one house at the western end of the green, possibly as old or older than Peare Tree House. Further to the west is the new Primitive Methodist Chapel and a little further on a bridge has been built over what was previously a ford across the beck. There was a smaller bridge, possibly wooden, a little further up the beck. Beyond Beech Tree Yard things look much as they do today. Another row of terraced cottages has been added, the ones put up by William Lawson for the farm workers. The sawmill is now marked and so is the mill-race from the sawmill to Mechi Farm. The building on the other side of the road has now disappeared, but a little further on a path leads to the house known as The Gardens, originally part of Mechi Farm. By 1925, the next Ordnance Survey map shows that the old smithy has gone and that a Sunday School has been set up on the north side of the east road.

The chief development during the twentieth century is, not surprisingly, that people live with more space and more comfort.

Dwellings which once consisted of two, three or four houses are now converted for the use of one family. Farm buildings, once attached to cottages, have been turned into living accommodation. The old outside lavatories and ashpits, usually set in a row opposite the houses they served, have either been removed, like the ones by the High Road in West Court, or else converted to other uses, like the many which survive at the western end of the village. The old trades and all but one of the shops have disappeared. There is now a garage close by where the smithy once stood, the sawmill has now been converted into a house, the cobbler's shop is used for storage but was once a popular place for people to meet and talk, especially when the cobbler was Bob Hanvey, who was also a rugby international. A wheelwright plied his trade at the far end of the village near East Farm, a tailor occupied one of four houses in what is now one house on the north side of the east road and a saddler worked in another; there have been two fish and chip shops, a sweetshop and a bakery. All of these, except the smithy, were here within the memory of some of the older members of the community.

The course of the River Ellen was altered in the 1950s. This river has been a constant source of flooding and no measures to stop it have been entirely successful. Drains have been sunk and flood banks raised. One of these is still visible, but much lower than it once was, in the field on the north side of the river. This field used to be known as Walker Garth and was on the border between Blennerhasset and Baggrow. People were always uncertain where the boundary ought to be and back in 1817, when the field was sold by Daniel Jackson, it was described as being 'in Baggrow or Blennerhasset'. During heavy rain the river still floods this field as well as the road between Baggrow and Blennerhasset, making it impassable and sometimes flooding houses at the north end of the village. There has been nothing recently though like the flood which within living memory inundated the terraced houses on the north side of the green.

There were to be three further developments which extended the reach of the village into the surrounding countryside. One was

The High Road with the council houses, built after the Second World War. The road runs on to meet the Carlisle-Cockermouth road.

the construction after the Second World War of some council houses along the High Road to the south. These, some of which are now privately owned, are far more attractive than the average council house and are set back from the road by well tended gardens. Another was the building of houses and bungalows along the north side of the back lonning and the third was the building of the Village Hall during the Second World War. Together with one recently built house on the last available space round the green and another house on the High Road these additions complete the shape of the village as it now stands

Mechi Farm

Mechi Farm is Blennerhasset's one claim to a small place in history. It is, ultimately, a tale of failure, of money squandered in the pursuit of an idealistic and over-ambitious venture which foundered on the (self-confessed) inexperience of its creator, William Lawson, the economic conditions of the time and the mute resistance of those he wanted to inspire. Yet the venture compels admiration, for its breadth of vision, its willingness to try out new methods and its results, which are still visible in the village today. The main source of information about the scheme can be found in *Ten Years of Gentleman Farming*, an account in which Lawson, and, for the later part of the book, his friend Charles Hunter, describe his achievements and all too frequent failures with commendable honesty[36].

William Lawson, son of Sir Wilfrid, was born in 1836 and had the typical upbringing of an English country gentleman on the

Above: The empty clock tower above the barns at Mechi Farm. The tower was damaged in a recent fire.

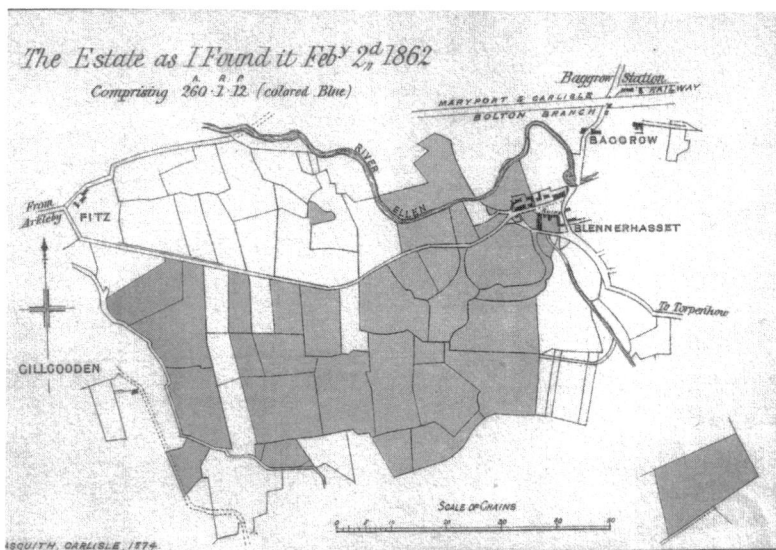

*"The Estate as I Found it Feby 2d, 1862". William Lawson's map
of the original Mechi farm.*

Brayton estate to the north of Baggrow. As he came to adulthood in
the early 1860s his father, already an important landowner, was in
the process of buying the estate of John Dawson, 260 acres,
including a water wheel powered by the extended mill-race
(presumably the one which serviced Dawson's threshing machine)
and the Lordship of the Manor. He also bought the estate of the
Hodgson family, then in the possession of Cornelius Robson of
Liverpool, who had married Mary, the last surviving descendant of
the family, and, a few years later, the Benson estate, 420 acres in all.
William, feeling he wanted more experience of the world than was
provided by his life at Brayton, had embarked on a tour which
brought him in 1861 to a farm in Essex operated on modern methods
by Alderman Mechi (hence the name of the Lawson farm). This was
the inspiration which led his father to convey the whole
Blennerhasset estate to him, together with enough capital to carry
out his schemes.

From then on, much of the land began to be transformed.

66

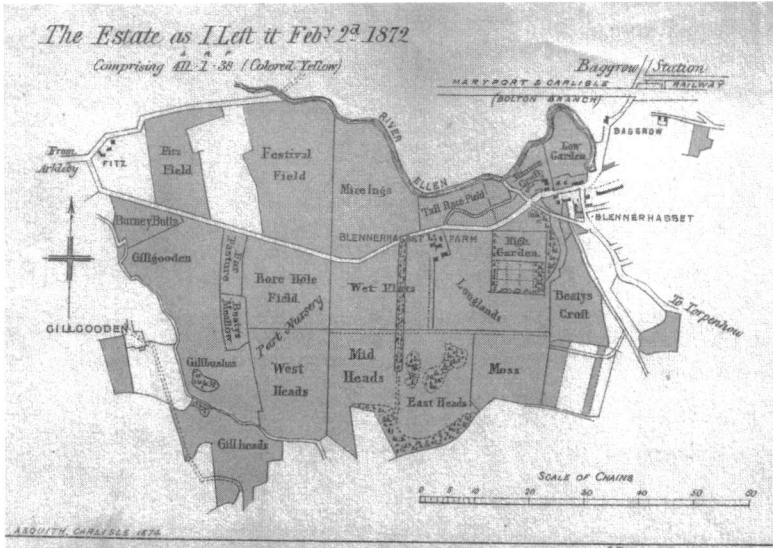

"The Estate as I Left it Feby 2d, 1872". William Lawson's map of the improvements he made at Mechi farm.

Hedges were grubbed up to create large fields out of the irregular shapes which had existed there before, roads were made, drains dug and impressive modern farm buildings - still there - were erected on a new site, including a tower with a turret clock with three faces, also still there, but damaged in a recent fire. No longer there is the 20 horse-power turbine water wheel. The old farm buildings, which faced the road, were partly converted into living accommodation for the farm workers, and there were plans to build new cottages. These were either converted from the old stables, byres and barns of the Dawson farm or else built from scratch. Four out of the five completely new cottages were built in one row at the west end of the village in 1866 and 1867 and, with the outhouses which were later added, were valued in 1870 at £132 7 0 each. The rent for these was fixed at 2/6 a week but there was a certain amount of dissatisfaction because they had no gardens, so a resolution was passed in the village parliament in 1868 that land should be provided for this purpose. A field was divided up (probably Wheat Close, on the north

67

Today many houses in the village have their gardens separate from the accommodation. Above is part of what was originally known as Wheat Close, and was allotted to the occupants of the newly-built houses by William Lawson.

side of the Arkleby road) and plots of land were rented out at 6s 4d per annum. This partly explains why today so many houses in the village have their gardens separate from the accommodation. The housing provided by the Mechi Farm scheme more or less completed the shape of the main part of the village as it stands today.

But the farm and the new cottages were far from being the limit of the experiment. William Lawson had big ideas and the main obstacle to their fulfilment, at least at the beginning, was the difficulty of arousing interest, still less cooperation, among the farm labourers. In the famous vote on which workers were asked whether they wanted a cooperative scheme or 'every man for himself', the vast majority, ten to one in fact, voted 'every man for himself'. Not that there is anything very surprising about this. Men who had known of nothing beyond the lives they had always led could not be expected to be filled with enthusiasm for the grandiose plans of the young son of the Lord of the Manor when he suddenly descended on them and wanted to change everything. Attitudes must have altered though, at least a little, when in 1866 profits began to be made and 10% of it went to the workers. Some of these profits came from 12 acres of market garden which sold produce not only locally but also in shops set up in Carlisle and Newcastle. The farm shop in the village still survives; workers were paid in specially minted coins which could be spent there. It was handed over to the People's Shop Company in 1872 when the scheme was wound up and became known as the People's Shop until, in 1926, Sir Wilfrid Lawson sold it and the adjoining terrace of cottages, known as Cross Cottages, to Joseph Blacklock.

Lawson did not allow himself to be discouraged by the resistance of the workers. His plan was to involve the whole village in the project and in 1866 an 'Open Council' was founded, known as the village parliament. It met weekly, on a Tuesday, in Beech House, and, apart from the gardens already mentioned, led to the establishment of free reading rooms, a free library, the Blennerhasset Free School and a night school. The library was surprisingly successful. By 1872 it contained 1,754 volumes and its most active year was 1871, when 2,340 loans were made. There was one dispute over its contents: this concerned the works of Thomas Paine which, despite the fact that he had died in 1809, were still regarded as dangerous and subversive. He had supported the French Revolution and one of his books, The Age of Reason, was known by some as 'the Atheist's Bible'. Paine was not in fact an atheist, but he did attack the Christian religion and this was enough to condemn him in the eyes of the dissenting (Congregational) minister and his followers. Although Lawson thought Paine's works should be kept, the minister carried the day and in 1871 they were burnt on the village green.

The free school was set up in 1867. A school already existed but an increase in population, partly because of the farm, led Lawson to propose free schooling for all. After some opposition, from the existing schoolmaster among others, the plan was finally agreed. A

The village post office still bears the coat of aems of Sir Wilfrid Wybergh Lawson.

schoolmistress from Inverness was appointed, and there were about 70 children on the roll, with an average attendance of about 50, though this figure went down when there was more work to be done in the fields. (Education was not made compulsory at elementary level until the 1880 Act). The free school was short-lived because the Education Act of 1870 established elementary schooling for all under locally elected school boards and the school closed the following year.

Another innovation was the Free Bath Room. Like other schemes, it was not pushed through until much discussion had taken place at the parliament, but it was finally set up in the winter of 1868-9 in a corner of the turnip house (the only bathroom in Britain to be located in a turnip house?). It boasted 'a spray, a douche, a wooden plunge bath and a packing trestle'. Unfortunately William Lawson's book does not explain what a packing trestle is. In any case the bathhouse, and the whole building, were destroyed in a fire in the summer of 1871 and were never rebuilt. The water for the baths was probably heated by the gas supply, a great technical development

One of the surviving gaslamps from William Lawson's scheme.

which began working in 1865. Gas was supplied to the village as well as the farm, but some of the villagers thought twice about the scheme when the quarterly bills began to come in and went back to their candles. The gas was also used to provide street lighting and two of the lampposts can still be seen in the village, one at the crossroads and another on the east road.

Perhaps the development which created the biggest stir in the neighbourhood was the adoption of a steam plough. In February 1862 No. 95 of Fowler's Patent Steam Ploughing Tackle arrived at Aspatria station, about two miles away, and with much effort was transported to the farm. It was not easy to operate, to say the least, and four years later a double-engine system was purchased, with an engine standing at each end of the field. They were christened Cain and Abel. Fifteen men were employed to operate these machines and earned, between them, £12.15.0 a week.

A list of individual wages made in 1870 gives some idea of

Above: Some of the houses which were built for Mechi farmworkers.
Below: The outhouses at the rear of the above used originally as
latrines and ash-pits.

the extent of the undertaking, as well as the relative importance attached to each occupation. The highest paid employee was the chemist who worked in the experimental laboratory and earned £2.2.0 a week. Next were the bailiff and his wife with £1.10.0. and then the clerk at £1.6.6. The only other workers earning more than a pound a week were the smith, who got £1.4.5¹/₂., and two joiners with £1.1.6 each. Also on the payroll were a time-keeper, a groom and two wallers. All of these were of course a cut above the ordinary farm labourers who were paid by the day. In the same year, 1870, men earned between 2/- and 3/2, women 1/3 but double at harvest time, boys 1/3 and girls 1/-. Altogether, 65 people were employed on the farm and another 18 in other departments.

Lawson was also anxious to provide his employees and the villagers with some enjoyment. To this end the Blennerhasset Festivals were organised at Christmas time. The first was in 1866 and was definitely not a success. The menu, without meat and the rest of it badly cooked because of the inadequate kitchen facilities, was not to the participants' liking, nor apparently to that of the pigs, who were given the leftovers. The next year beef was provided, everything was properly cooked and the 1,000 people who attended seem to have been well satisfied. The 1868 event was even more ambitious with beef, ham, oranges, apples, lemonade (this was a temperance party) soup and rice pudding, for which 16 stone of rice was bought. There were also lectures, eleven in number, which could hardly have contributed to the party spirit, but were certainly in the very Victorian spirit of Lawson's enterprise, to improve and educate. Some of the lecture titles were: 'Practical Education and Training', 'Phrenology, illustrated by character sketches of some of the audience' and 'The Nation's Highest Good'. The festivals were by now being reported in the national press, including *The Times* and *Punch*. Blennerhasset was briefly on the map. The year 1869 saw the last of these Christmas festivals. This time there were only two invited speakers and three local ones, but lectures still went on throughout the day and there was dancing 'in the Dancing Hall, where strict order will be maintained'. The last festival was held in the summer, after which the parliament decided against having any more.

An interesting feature of the 1869 festival was that, among the musical items, performed on harmonium and violin, was the French National Anthem, the Marseillaise. This was not the only sign of interest in what was happening in France, where the Franco-Prussian War was soon to break out. When the profits were distributed in 1868, the remainder, after the workers were rewarded, was sent to the Aspatria Cottage Hospital Fund, which decided the next year to send it to help the wounded soldiers in France. A local dignitary, George Moore, of White Hall (where the Salkelds had lived) was also very much involved in the events in France and went out to help during the war. Even before the war broke out, Lawson had made a visit to the Paris International Exhibition in 1867 and made £60 available for people to go to the Exhibition. £3 was offered to every male worker and £4.10.0 to every female worker who wanted to go. His motive in being more generous to the women than to the men is not explained; perhaps he thought that the women would enjoy spending money more, but a more likely explanation, considering the temperance tradition in the Lawson family, is that he thought the men would probably only spend the extra money on drink. Applicants had to be recommended by the village parliament. It's a pity that no record is available of how they enjoyed their visit.

One other annual event, and possibly the most enjoyable for those involved, was the trip to Keswick. About 40 or 50 workers would set out at 4 or 5 o'clock in the morning in farm carts and reach Keswick about 10 o'clock. After a day 'at leisure' they would leave about 5 o'clock and get back around midnight, pausing occasionally on the way for a dance, if they had a fiddler with them.

But by 1871 it became clear that the scheme could not go on. Too many aspects of the farming operation were unprofitable and the estate was sold off. No record remains of how the people of Blennerhasset felt about it all, but their lives could not have been the same again. Horizons had been broadened: the possibilities of advanced farming methods were opened up and people became aware, in thought and action, of a world beyond the confines of village life. With hindsight, the project looks like an uneasy combination of socialism and Victorian paternalism, democratic cooperation and benevolent management from above. Today, with the exception of the new buildings on the farm and in the village, it is as though it had never been, but those buildings are a permanent reminder that Blennerhasset once had, all those years ago, its brief moment of glory.

Transport

As we have seen, the farm workers who went for their outing to Keswick travelled in farm carts. For most individuals of course the only way of getting from one place to another was to walk, and the many farm labourers who changed jobs every few years would have walked in search of the next one, carrying their meagre possessions with them. The better off would have hired, or even owned, a horse, or a horse and carriage, and for longer distances there was the stage coach. These ran from inns or similar establishments, mostly in the bigger towns such as Carlisle, where in 1774 'a new post coach on steel springs' was announced in the Cumberland Pacquet. It took three days to get to London, starting from Beck's Coffee House on Sundays, Tuesdays and Thursdays. The fare for an inside passenger was £3.10.0, half price for outside passengers; 'children on the lap' could travel for nothing. In the following year

Above: A horse and cart making an appearance at a village show a hundred years or so ago.

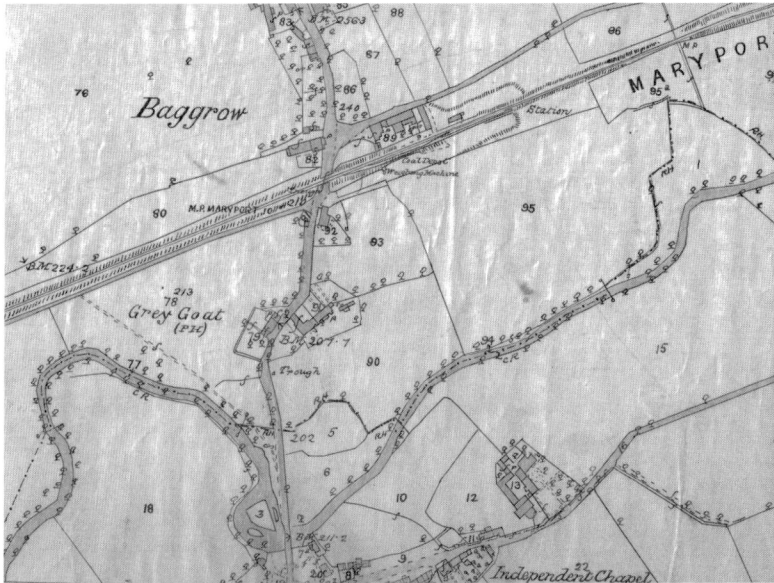

The railway line running on the far side of the River Ellen through Baggrow.

the enterprising publican, Mr Ferdinando Johnston, at the Coach and Horses, Cockbridge, a small village on the Carlisle-Cockermouth road near the turning to Blennerhasset, announced the enlargement of his premises and a 'Neat Post Chaise'. Mr Johnston could not have enjoyed the profits from this service for long though, as the Inn and its 42 acres are advertised to let later in the same year by John Dixon of Whitehall.

In 1797 there was yet another announcement, this time of a Post Coach from the Blue Bell Inn, Carlisle, leaving at 8 a.m. on Tuesdays, Thursdays and Saturdays. On the first day you arrived at Lancaster at 7 p.m., left at 7.00 the following morning for Liverpool, arriving at 5 p.m. and changing coaches here for London, Bath or Bristol. As well as the usual fares for inside and outside there was another schedule for 'short passengers, inside 4d per mile'. Despite what it looks like, this of course refers to the length of the journey, not the traveller.

77

Many of the roads required tolls to be paid, including the one through the Brayton estate north of Blennerhasset and Baggrow. In 1825 there was a new toll on the turnpike road from Carlisle to Cockermouth. 'For every horse, mule, ass, or other beast drawing any coach, landau, berlin, phaeton, curricle, chariot, chaise, calash, hearse, caravan, gig, chair, car or other carriage, the sum of four pence.' Only mail coaches were exempted from the toll. Most of these vehicles would be privately owned, but the coach and chaise were for public use. The coach was the larger of the two, with, as we have seen, seats inside and out; the chaise seated three passengers at the most, and the driver sat on one of the horses. The car is a slightly surprising vehicle to find itself in the list at this time, but in those days it was a general term for a cheap means of transport, a carriage, wagon or carrier cart (popularly known as a 'clog cart') on which one could travel locally for a small sum.

Later years saw the coming of the pony and trap, and cars, the modern type, began to replace the horse at the turn of the century. They must have been seen, if not owned, in Blennerhasset in the early twentieth century, but for the first solid evidence we have to wait until 1917, when the Headmaster of Blennerhasset School comments disapprovingly in his log book on 'various boys throwing sods and running after vehicles and motor cars, stone throwing'. In the earlier part of the century there were regular bus services through the village, but nowadays the bus calls only rarely, since nearly every household owns one, two or more cars.

Blennerhasset Mill

At some distance to the north of the township, where the River Ellen forms its boundary, lies a sandstone flour-mill. It is known to have been working in the mid-seventeenth century, grinding corn for the people of Blennerhasset and Baggrow, and is almost certainly much older. It was still in working order around 1930 but had already stopped producing corn, probably unable to compete with the great steam mill at Silloth, which was set up at the beginning of the twentieth century, but it may have ceased activity even before that, judging from the occupations of the last two tenants recorded in the census. In 1842 John Fell is recorded as being the owner of 'Mill Garth Race and Premises' as well as four

The millrace. The millwheel has not yet been restored but most of the materials have already been acquired.

Ore of the mill buildings

fields around it, the largest of which, Mill Crook, occupied the land adjoining the bend in the river. By 1879 the estate was owned by William Fletcher but from at least 1861 the mill was occupied by the Barnes family. The 1881 census records Elizabeth Barnes, widow, 56, as being a miller and farmer of 50 acres, rather more than was owned by John Fell. In 1891 we find another Barnes, Joseph, aged 24, listed as a farm labourer, and in 1901 Richard Lawson, miner hewer, and his wife and son, also a miner, aged 14, so it seems unlikely that these two would have operated the mill.

Today the site is occupied by Andy Curle, who, with the help of volunteers, has begun the huge task of restoring it. Most of the materials are ready for the rebuilding of the mill-wheel, the mill-house has been made secure and work has already taken place to make the site self-sufficient with electricity generators operated by a water turbine (the mill is not in any case linked to the national grid), solar panels, compost toilets and an organic farm. The whole project is intended to show the possibility of leading a life which does not spoil the planet.

Churches

For a long period the only church available for the inhabitants of Blennerhasset lay two miles away in Torpenhow and it therefore played a large part in the lives of the villagers. Blennerhasset baptisms, marriages and burials are regularly recorded in the church register[37], though not everyone chose to have their ceremonies at Torpenhow. A number of Blennerhasset baptisms, marriages and burials also appear in the Register for Allhallows, including families such as the Hodgsons, the Gunsons and the Winders. Allhallows church, dating from 1587, was restored by George Moore, of nearby Whitehall, in 1862. It now lies in ruins, apart from the Norman chancel, and a new church was built along the main road and completed in 1899. The amount of detail in the Register seems to have depended on the conscientiousness of those who drew it up. Sometimes we find just the names of those concerned, at others, social status and profession are recorded: yeoman, farmer, poor householder, boarder. The Allhallows Register was quite explicit about the origins of the children baptised[38]. In 1754 it records the baptism of 'William, the Bastard Son of Jane Thompson'. Perhaps in

Above: The old Congregational Chapel, now a private house.

this case the identity of the father was not known, but sometimes it was. Three years later we find 'Joseph, a Bastard Son of Philip Waller, by Mary Nut'. In the earliest registers available from Torpenhow, for the seventeenth century, the village seems to have been full of Bouches and Atkinsons, later to be joined by Jacksons, Hodgsons and Martindales, and the old spellings are still there: 'Blenrasset' and 'Aspatricke'.

The church at that time had an important role in the government of the parish. The Sixteen, already mentioned in the section on 'The Poor', acted as parish council and school governors and also carried out a number of administrative functions which would today be the responsibility of a district council. Some of what they did is recorded in the Torpenhow Churchwardens' and Vestry Book[39]. Here we learn that in 1756 the Sixteen, together with the vicar, investigated complaints about the schoolmaster. He was accused of immoral behaviour and neglect of the school and was told that he must improve his ways and 'keep the school' from seven to eleven in the morning and one to six in the afternoon from Lady Day (25 March) to Michaelmas (29 September) and from nine to twelve and from one to three from Michaelmas to Lady Day. In 1776 it was decided that in future the Sixteen would be responsible for choosing the schoolmaster by majority vote. The present one was deemed 'an improper person to be continued'. As the schoolmaster's name is not mentioned it is not clear whether this is the same one who had caused dissatisfaction before but had somehow managed to hang on to the job for another twenty years, or another, perhaps equally unsatisfactory incumbent. From now on the post was to be occupied by the Reverend Richard Hair, whose occupation surely made him a safer bet. He was to receive 1/- a quarter 'for every child not a poor person's child', 1/6 if they were taught writing and 2/- if they were taught arithmetic or Latin and Greek.

The Sixteen, represented by the churchwarden, were also responsible for recording the value, owners and occupiers of property so that Land Tax and the Poor Rate could be assessed and distributed and also the names of those eligible for service in the

Militia. Accounts were also kept of their income and expenditure. The most interesting item from these is an annual payment of 5/- made to the sexton between 1810 and 1812 'for driving Dogs out of the Church'. The church at Torpenhow thus affected everybody's lives, even dogs, in a material way, but not necessarily in a spiritual one.

Resistance to the established church was traditionally strong in the north of the country. When Henry VIII dissolved the monasteries objectors from Lincolnshire to Cumberland joined the Pilgrimage of Grace (1536-7) which seriously challenged the king's power. This was a case of Roman Catholics challenging the power of what would later become the Anglican Church. The king at first made efforts to come to terms with the rebels, but as resistance weakened he brutally repressed what remained of the movement. The Pilgrimage deserves a mention here because a man was publicly hanged in Torpenhow for joining it. Refusal to accept the religious authority of the church later took shape in various movements of dissent, beginning with the Presbyterians, later to be joined by the Independents or Congregationalists (who dissented from the Presbyterians), the Baptists, the Quakers and, in the eighteenth century, the Methodists.

Dissenters and Catholics had a difficult time under the Anglican Church. It was only in 1828 that non-members of the Anglican Church finally gained something like equal rights. In the seventeenth century priests, or their churchwardens, were required to report those who failed to attend church to the ecclesiastical courts. These reports were known as 'presentments' and began with the words 'we present'. In 1682 the vicar of Allhallows, quite coura- geously, seeing that he was Lord of the Manor, presented 'Sir Francis Salkeld, Lady Anne his wife and Thomas Salkeld Esqre, convicted papists'[40]. The religious convictions of the many other names presented are not given, nor do we know what punishment, if any, they suffered, but it is quite likely that some of these non- attenders would have been members of the Presbyterian Church who, before the foundation of the Blennerhasset chapel, would have

The last church to be built in Blennerhasset. Originally built for the Primitive Methodists, it is now called the Evangelical Mission. It is constructed in that style affectionately known as the 'tin tabernacle'.

attended the church in Cockermouth, which was formed as early as 1661.

There is no record of the original granting of a licence to the independent church in Blennerhasset but we do know that it was revoked on 12 July, 1704[41]. A few days later an entry in the Presbyterian Church records reads: '17th July 1704 in the morning John Wallas of Threepld and another dissenter desiring Restitution of the licenced house in Blennerhasset and both confessed to employing preachers of difference persuasions' [i.e. non-Anglican]. Restitution must have been granted at some time because on 17th March, 1714, the minutes of the Presbyterian Fund Board tell us that a grant of £8 was made to a Mr Stewart of Blennerhasset. He is the first known minister. Most of the early ministers came from Scotland. Worship seems to have continued steadily there throughout the eighteenth century but at the beginning of the nineteenth the chapel fell into disuse except for an occasional visit by a minister from Wigton. It was rebuilt in 1828 as a Congregational chapel with the help of a £100 gift from George Dawson, soon to become Lord of the Manor. There was accommodation for 140 worshippers and it enjoyed a regular series of ministers until 1857 after which there were few services until it closed in 1864. It was then that a new manse was built 'as a residence for the Minister for the time being of the Protestant Dissenters at Blennerhasset'. The land was donated by Sir Wilfrid Lawson on the site formerly known as Peile's Croft on the south side of the Green. Exactly a hundred years later the manse was sold by the Lancashire Congregational Union as a private dwelling house.

Congregationalists could not have been the only dissenters, or non-conformists, to use the present-day term, in the village. The main guide to religious worship in the mid-nineteenth century is the Census of Religious Worship of 1851[42]. This was a national survey and deals only with districts, not individual towns and villages. Judging by the figures for the Wigton area, the highest numbers of dissenting churches were 8 Wesleyan Methodist followed by 7 Congregational and 6 Quaker; all these denominations could have had followers in the village. Attendance figures show that the Congregational churches had more regular worshippers than the Methodist and a far higher proportion, in terms of numbers of churches and worshippers, than the Anglican churches, where the Census revealed shockingly low attendance figures.

Another denomination which must have been represented in the village were the Primitive Methodists, for whom only two churches appear in the Census. A legal document of 1883 records the lease 'of a plot of ground at Blennerhasset intended as a site for an Iron Chapel' for the 'Members and Friends of the Primitive Methodist Connection'[43]. This was consented to by the occupiers of the plot, Messrs Fletcher & Co., colliery proprietors. The lease was for a term of 21 years, the rent 2/6 per annum. The Primitive Methodists were a breakaway group from the Wesleyan Methodists and adopted a down-to-earth, revivalist style of preaching more to the taste of working people than the more formal services of the Wesleyans. They had a teetotal tradition which no doubt appealed to Sir Wilfrid Lawson, who arranged the lease and secured the services of the Reverend Ralph Shields, a Primitive Methodist minister from Wigton. The 'prims' flourished in the mining areas and the church probably owed its foundation to the large numbers of miners then living in the village.

Mines

The Mechi experiment is one thing that has come and gone in Blennerhasset; another is the mining community. Unlike many local villages which came into being to service the pits and whose rows of identical terraced houses bear permanent witness to their origins, Blennerhasset was well established as a farming village before the coming of the miners and lived on after their departure without a trace of their ever having been there. No extra accommodation seems to have been built for them; they simply found homes or lodgings in the village as it stood. In many cases houses must have been split into two or more living areas to accommodate them, which would explain the apparent increase in dwellings recorded in the censuses of the period when no further houses seem to have been built.

We know from the census the names of the miners who lived in Blennerhasset in the last third of the nineteenth century but there

Above: Miners waiting to go up in the cage in No. 5 Pit of the Brayton Domain collieries.

87

At the coal face.

is of course no indication of which mine they actually worked at. We can only assume that they made their way to the various pits which lay nearest to the village[44]. The largest mining area was the Brayton Domain Colliery, two miles away near Aspatria. It belonged to Sir Wilfrid Lawson and was leased to John Harris of Greysouthen. The first pits, Nos 1 and 2, were sunk there in 1850, and from then on further pits were sunk at intervals until the early twentieth century, No 3 pit at Harriston in 1868, followed by No 4 (near the Carlisle road) in 1888 and No 5 (near the Station) in 1907. Aspatria Station had its own coal depot, as well as cattle pens. The Brayton Domain Colliery having the advantage of being close to the Maryport and Carlisle railway, the pits were highly successful. During the First World War Nos 4 and 5 pits employed 900 men with an annual production of 200,000 tons. No 4 closed down in 1933 and No 5 carried on into the Second World War, shutting down in 1942.

Joseph Harris, perhaps the son of the John Harris already mentioned, took a twenty-one year lease in 1881 from Sir Wilfrid of several mines in the area, including one at Allhallows. There were already pits in this area operated by Messrs I. & W. Fletcher, and

No 4 Pit

some of the Blennerhasset miners must have been employed there. Closer to Blennerhasset was the Brayton Knowe pit, in the field on the opposite side of the road from the house in Baggrow known as The Knowe. This, operated by the Allerdale Coal Company, was not active until 1902, though its presence is already recorded on the Ordnance Survey map of 1900. It was not particularly productive and closed for good in 1918, with many of the miners finding jobs at the pits at Allhallows and Brayton. Apart from a gas explosion at one of the Allhallows pits in 1877, when one miner was killed, there do not seem to have been any serious incidents at the local pits.

Miners' pay varied considerably during the period when the mines were active. In the mid-nineteenth century the average was 2/6 to 3/- a day, a shilling less than in the other northern counties, mainly because wages were depressed by the influx of immigrants, mostly from Ireland but also from Scotland. By the early 1870s pay had shot up to 7/-, through the shortage of labour resulting from the expansion of the iron industry. But this was not to last: in 1874 a fall in the price of coal led to a 10% cut in wages. The workers at No 3 pit at Brayton went on strike for six weeks, during which time wages were cut by a further 15%. This resulted in widespread strikes going on into the next year. It was during this troubled period that the mining population of Blennerhasset was beginning to grow. Wages had fallen back in the eighties to between 2/9 and 4/-, with boys earning between 1/- and 2/9 and women between 1/- and 1/6.

Although miners were generally better paid than agricultural workers, Cumberland miners were consistently worse off than in other northern counties. This was again the case after the national coal strikes of 1912, which resulted in wages being fixed by a joint board for each district. Then Cumberland miners were awarded much less than the national average. Conditions improved during the First World War but then steadily worsened until Cumberland and Westmorland were declared a Special Area during the depression of 1928-38. In the General Strike of 1926 most of the working population went back to work after four days, but the miners carried on for nearly eight months. By this time the number of miners in the village had diminished considerably, but there was still enough hardship for some families to benefit from the Lord Mayor's Fund of 1929, which allocated £5 for children at Blennerhasset School who were in need of clothing and footwear[45]. During a further coal strike in 1931, the situation was considered serious enough for free meals to be provided for children at the school. This would have applied not just to the children of striking miners but also to those whose fathers were in any case unemployed owing to the depressed state of the economy. In the November of that year the school was required to supply details of children who were thought to be suffering from malnutrition so that they could be provided with free milk.

The village must have been severely overcrowded while the miners were there, but they certainly made their mark on village life. It's worth remembering that in those days, when the vast majority of families could not afford to send their children to secondary school, many men of considerable intellect and ability were obliged to work in the mines because there was simply no alternative. As we shall see, all kinds of activities were pursued, sport flourished and some miners, such as John Dial and Richard Graham, became property owners. Graham bought a house on the High Road, just south of East Terrace and another piece of land south of that, and Dial bought a house in East Terrace. Both sales took place in 1908, two years after the death of Sir Wilfrid Lawson, the former owner. As with all houses sold by Lawson, the buyers had to sign a covenant not to use the house or premises for the sale of liquor. John Dial was also one of the managers of the school for several years and in 1897 became Chairman. By the early 1930s the miners had gone, and the village began to take the form which it has had ever since.

With the running down of the mines came the eventual abandonment of the railway which served them. It was a branch of the Carlisle-Maryport railway, started in the 1860s to enable more coal shipments to be made from Maryport. It was a loop, branching off from the main line at Aikbank Junction and running through Baggrow where the station, as well as serving as a coal depot, provided cattle pens; it then joined up with the main line again at Aspatria. This line was used to transport coal to Maryport and in the other direction carried goods to Carlisle, including produce from Mechi farm. In later years the railway would take on some passenger coaches once a year and run a special trip.

The Bolton Loop and the mines.

The Bolton Loop was established to service the mines in the area. So called because a good part of the line ran through the villages known collectively as the Boltons, it ran from Aspatria to Aikbank and there were three stations, Baggrow, Mealsgate and High Blaithwaite. There was a further narrow gauge line running from Aspatria to Harriston and then on to the limestone quarry at Plumbland. The section from Aspatria to Mealsgate opened in 1866 and the rest of the line to Aikbank was completed in 1878.

The loop was run by the same company that operated the main Maryport and Carlisle line and functioned in two parts, Aspatria to Mealsgate and Mealsgate to Wigton. The Aspatria section was much the busier of the two with five trains a day against the one a day in the other section, which closed down in 1921. The Aspatria section ran passenger trains until 1930 and goods trains, plus one passenger train a week, until 1952, but the main purpose of the loop was always to serve the mining industry. The line closed officially in 1953.

In fact there had been pits in the Bolton and Mealsgate area since the seventeenth century but mining only began to develop on a large scale in the nineteenth century. Nearer to Blennerhasset, Allhallows Colliery was sunk in 1874 and was enlarged in 1886 but the nearest pit to Blennerhasset was the Brayton Knowe Colliery which opened in 1902 and closed in 1918. At that time 119 men worked underground and 45 above. All these pits used the railway to transport their coal but the main user of the line was the Brayton Domain Colliery. Here, as described in the section on mines in the main text, the various pits, five in all, were worked from 1850 until 1942. The Brayton Domain always did better because it enjoyed cheaper rates on the railway. The miners of Blennerhasset could well have worked in all these pits. The only positive evidence I have found of where they worked comes from the log book kept by the headmaster of the school, John Stephenson. The entry for 12 August, 1918, reports that the colliery at Baggrow has now closed for good, but that some of the miners have already found employment at Allhallows and Brayton.

Social Life

The earliest record of any social life in the village has already been mentioned in the account of Mechi Farm. After that the use of the School for social events, recorded in the minutes and log books[45], gives some idea of the range of activities pursued in the later years of the nineteenth century and early in the twentieth. Most of the societies and clubs liked to have an Annual Ball, and the only place they could have them was in the School. The word 'Ball' doesn't necessarily mean that these events were very grand affairs, but they certainly seem to have been fairly lively and the users were not too careful about how they treated school property. For a Cricket Club Ball held in 1894, for which the hall was booked from 7.30

Above: The village carnival procession in 1912 passing in front of Cross Cottages.

James William Lowther opening the 1912 Carnival. Judging from the way the people are wrapped up, the weather could not have been very warm.

James Lowther (1855-1949) was Unionist M.P. for Penrith from 1886 to 1921 and was Speaker of the House of Commons from 1905 to 1921. He was knighted and created 1st Viscount Ullswater in 1921. He was the author of the famous advice to Parliamentary speakers: "Stand up. Speak up. Shut up."

until 6.30 the next morning, the members were particularly requested not to abuse the school furniture, but, sure enough, a request was later made by the school managers that the Club should make good the damage caused to school furniture. A booking until 6.30 in the morning was rare, but dances regularly went on into the small hours. Even the Congregational Committee could not be trusted, it seems. A letter was written in 1890 to the Reverend M.Potts, the Minister, complaining about the state of the schoolroom after its meeting. And a Conservative whist drive managed to break a thermometer.

Other meetings and balls were held by the Blennerhasset Football Club (sometimes enlivened by the Blennerhasset String Band) and the Blennerhasset Reading Society, which on one

94

Girls with bicycles at the 1912 carnival got up to represent the seasons.

Below: an obliging donkey leads the parade almost a century ago.

Lower picture: From a Carnival about forty years ago. Gladys Bowen, Dorothy Relph, Jennifer Blacklock (now in Australia), Miss Lawson (schoolteacher), Martha Turner.

Above and opposite: Further images of village merry-making throughout the last century.

occasion hired the schoolroom until 4 o'clock, and on another was entertained by the Brayton Minstrels. At a more spiritual level, the schoolroom was hired each year, well into the 1920s, to celebrate the anniversary of the Primitive Methodists, and the Temperance movement was represented by the Band of Hope. Older readers may remember being persuaded at these meetings to sign a pledge never to touch alcohol, a pledge which could hardly be considered binding when the subjects were probably no more than eight or nine years old. An application was also made by the Mealsgate Rechabite Brass Band; this was turned down. The Rechabites, well known at the time, were another Temperance group.

The schoolroom also hosted political meetings (usually Liberal), the Flower Show committee, continuation classes in ambulance, cookery and poultry farming, the Blennerhasset Poultry

An enthusiastic game of cricket between the sexes a half century or more ago.

and Pigeon Society, the Homing Pigeon Society, the Mechanics Society, the Aspatria Rifle Corps (for drill - no shots were fired, it seems), harvest thanksgiving sales and, during the Depression in the thirties, the Unemployed Club. In 1902, the Coronation committee met to prepare for the celebrations for King Edward VII's Coronation. Another initiative, by the Congregational minister, was the 'Pleasant Sunday Afternoons for the People'. There is no evidence of what went on at these gatherings, but they must have been a success, for they continued for some years. Possibly the first films seen in the village were shown at the Cinema Exhibition in 1925. It seems to have been quite exciting, as the Head Teacher found the school 'in a most filthy condition' the next morning, so much so that he sent the children home and closed the school for cleaning.

As the twentieth century progressed social life continued to be vigorously pursued. The Carnival was held annually until about 1980. The photos shown here suggest that in 1912 it was quite an

The Noddy Float, Carnival of 1978. The last carnival was held about 1980. Rosalie Rawlinson, Anne Jones, Lorraine Bowe. Policeman Plod has not been identified.

important event, important enough to be opened by the Speaker of the House of Commons, James Lowther. The procession came down the hill from Baggrow and then circled Blennerhasset. In fact the villagers would have had plenty of time on their hands in that year, when there was the long-lasting national coal strike.

Firework night was regularly celebrated, at first with a huge bonfire on the village green, but when the green began to be more carefully preserved, the fire was transferred to a site near the river. Judging from *The Cumberland Pacquet* of 1789, there was, long ago, a period when firework night was abandoned: 'The ridiculous and dangerous observance of the gunpowder-plot, by fire-works, &c. (to the credit of the present times) is universally laid aside. It was certainly the most absurd form of thanksgiving - for a deliverance from fire - that ever was adopted'. But then there had been something else to celebrate the year before, also on 5

November, and that was the centenary of the Glorious Revolution of 1688, which, with the landing on these shores of William and Mary, finally put an end to the threat that Britain might become a Catholic country. In Whitehaven the event was marked by salutes from cannons, 'Flights of Rockets, Shells, Tourbillons, Caskades of Fire, Blazing Stars, Mines, Powder, Grates, Garlands, Emblems, Sheaves and Roman Candles'. There were similar celebrations in other towns, perhaps equally imaginative, and dangerous.

An oddly named event which took place during the closing years of the nineteenth century and the beginning of the twentieth was 'Cousin Charley's Day'. The Blennerhasset School records show that a full day's holiday was granted by the School Board on that day, round about the beginning of May, for five successive years, 1898 to 1902. An article in a recent copy of *The Times and Star*[46] throws some more light on the 1898 celebration, to give it its full title: 'Cousin Charley's Children's Carnival and May Festival'. The site chosen for that year was Cockermouth and people flocked in from all the surrounding towns and villages. Cousin Charley was in fact James Bleasdale, editor of *The West Cumberland Times*, who had gathered together an impressive list of distinguished sponsors. The event was marked by a grand procession with brass bands, the crowning of the May Queen, athletic events, an operetta performed by the pupils of the Wigton National School and finally a firework display. The School records show that the 1900 celebration was held in Workington, but do not indicate any site for the remaining ones.

A meet of the Cumberland Foxhounds in the 1950s in front of the shop.

Education

The first hint of a school in Blennerhasset is contained in a letter to George Dawson from William Donald in September 1827[47]: 'There has been a great deal of altercation and disturbance respecting the Foundation of a School House upon the Waste Land at Blennerhasset, and it now devolves upon you to say, whether it has to be erected upon the present Foundation or not, you have already I am led to suppose seen the Foundation laid, and Mr Jackson and Mr Fell are now at my Elbow, and they, together with myself... will feel much obliged to you for an immediate answer to say whether we are to have it erected upon the present situation or not.'

Mr Dawson was, as we have seen, a cautious man where money matters were concerned and replied to say that he had no objection but that the consent of the freeholders ought to be

Above:A picture from before the First World War of the girls from the school. At that time there were always over a hundred children attending.

obtained. It appeared that Mr Ritson 'objected to have it built on the spot marked out' and so why did they not wait until next Spring 'as the proper season for building is so far advanced'. And that is all. There is no indication of where the waste land might be, but it's quite likely that it was roughly where the school is now, as Mr Ritson, the objector, at that time owned land right next to it, a two-acre field to the north of the houses at the east end of the village and stretching down to the river.

The main school in the parish at that time was in Bothel and it is probable that those children who went to school at all would have gone there. The Bothel endowed school had existed for centuries and was made free for poor children in 1686, others having to pay 2s.6d a quarter. The presence of a schoolmaster in Blennerhasset is recorded in 1829[48], and there was another in 1847[49] but no indication is given of where they worked. There is no positive evidence of a school in Blennerhasset until 1857. The log book of 1952 contains the tantalising information that during building work a bottle was discovered containing the history of the school from 1857 to 1911 and that a facsimile could be found in the log book. No such facsimile is there now and the bottle was replaced, we know not where, but it is presumably still somewhere under the floorboards waiting to be rediscovered. The first Ordnance Survey map, of 1865, definitely shows the school building, but rather smaller than it is now. This building probably housed the 'British School', where two teachers are recorded in the 1861 census, Jonathan Sharpe and his wife Eliza. British schools were being established all over the country following the 'Lancasterian system'. Pupils were taught in one schoolroom under the general supervision of the head teacher assisted by junior teachers. The fact that parents had to pay fees encouraged William Lawson of Mechi farm to set up a Free School [see section on Mechi Farm]. This was first proposed in 1866, but there was some opposition, coming partly from the existing British School teacher, and the matter was dropped, but Lawson did establish a night school, where the teaching was done by volunteers. With typical persistence, he revived the subject of a day school the

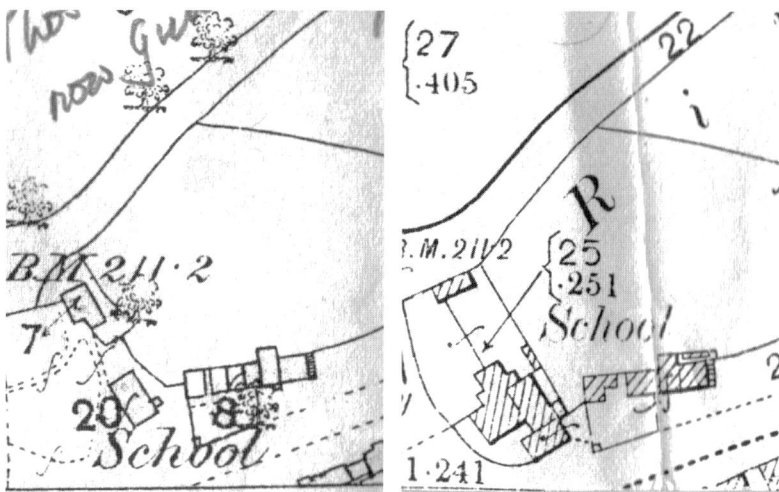

These two maps from 1865 and 1900 show how the school buildings changed in the nineteenth century.

following year and this time was successful. A teacher from Inverness was appointed and lessons began towards the end of 1867 with about 70 children on the roll.

Meanwhile the British School continued its work. The original schoolmaster had died quite young and the teaching was carried on by his son and daughter. There was still concern in the village about the existence of two schools and the question was raised whether the Free School should also be run by the British School teacher. After much debate in the village parliament a vote was held. 92 votes were cast for the Free School teacher and 65 for the British School teacher, the highest turnout ever in the parliament's brief history. So both schools continued side by side until the problem was taken out of their hands not long afterwards by the 1870 Act, which established elementary education for all children. The Free School closed in 1871 and, thanks to the efforts of Miss Lawson, the British School was made available free to all those children whose parents could not afford to pay for them.

The earliest Admissions Register for the school goes back to

A photo of the school from the early years of the twentieth century.

1867 and a few years later numbers on the roll began to increase quite rapidly with the influx of the children who had formerly attended William Lawson's Free School. Numbers fluctuated a lot, 97 being the highest figure for the 1870s. In those years children came from quite a distance to attend, including some from Aspatria, Watch Hill, Langrigg and Crookdake. One child lived at Aspatria No 2 Pit. As the population of the village grew, mostly thanks to the mines, so did the numbers at the school. Average attendance in 1894 was 165 and numbers were always above 100 until well into the twentieth century. Teaching was the responsibility of the Master, who enjoyed free accommodation in the School House next door and an annual salary of £100. With so many children to teach, he was constantly pressing for more help. Elementary education at this time was organised by assistant teachers, pupil teachers and monitors, the lower grades being appointed straight from the classroom. In 1885 a teacher from Wigton was appointed for the infants and also to teach

'Group 1', some of the younger pupils posing in front of the school in Edwardian times. This may be the lowest of the junior classes. Note the Eton collatrs worn by some of the boys.

singing and help with sewing. She earned £35 per annum and a 'monitress' was taken on at £8 per annum. In the same year the school decided to purchase the land down to the river for a new classroom and playground. There was no doubt that more space was sorely needed, with the Master complaining at one point of the difficulty of teaching seven standards (as classes were then called) in one room.

In the early years of the school parents had to pay for education unless they could show that they could not afford it. In 1886 a new reduced rate was introduced: 2d per week for children under 8, 4d between 8 and 10 and 5d for those above 10. Parents also had to buy their children's books. Only in 1891 did education at the school become entirely free in accordance with the Education Act of 1880. In those days a child's experience of school was very different from what it is today. As well as the usual reading, writing and arithmetic, much emphasis was laid on singing, reciting, drill and

The school today

religious instruction and the girls spent a lot of their time learning to sew. The children did their written work with chalk on slates, sponging off what they had written ready for the next lesson.

Towards the end of the nineteenth century there was another small school in the village. The only mention of it in the school records is a request that the lady in charge should provide a register of pupils. This she refused to do. The school is probably the one that was accommodated in the Manse. Little is known about it. It was very likely a `Dame School' for younger children, charging fees for tuition.

From the late nineteenth century on the school seems to have flourished. Inspectors' reports, it's true, were not always complimentary about the progress of the older children. Attendance was a problem, with parents often needing children to stay away for the harvest and such other tasks as turnip thinning and potato lifting. In

Girls from the school, apparently dressed up for carnival. If this is the famous 1912 carnival, the gentleman in the middle, who looks as if he would rather not be in the picture, may be the Headmaster, Mr Stephenson.

1902 the School Board craftily moved the school holidays to turnip-thinning time so as to boost the attendance record. Those who were nearing the end of their school career often lost any enthusiasm they might once have had and saw no need to attend every day of the week.

From time to time outside events affected the school. Flooding of the River Ellen regularly meant that children from Baggrow were unable to get to school, or else they arrived so wet that they were sent home again. In 1900 the scholars subscribed 15/- to the War Fund for the Boer War and further subscriptions were made during the First and Second World Wars. Epidemics, mostly of measles and chicken pox, would sometimes cause the school to be closed, but the longest closure was one of nine weeks for the great influenza epidemic at the end of the First World War which caused the deaths of two of the children. The Second World War saw the arrival of the evacuees, thirteen from South Shields and seven from Newcastle. Despite a boost in numbers from Newcastle in 1940,

The River Ellen in flood

their numbers slowly diminished and hardly any saw the war out at Blennerhasset.

1951 saw the only mention the school was ever to receive in the national press. The enterprising Headmaster, Mr Braithwaite, took a party to London for the Festival of Britain exhibition and while there they attended the burial of the ashes of Ernest Bevin, the former Foreign Secretary, at Westminster Abbey. A report from The Daily Telegraph reads. 'Children from the village school of Blennerhasset, Cumberland, on a Festival visit to London, attended the service. At its close, the children filed past the grave.' In 1953 the school was the only one in Cumberland to send children to see the Coronation of Queen Elizabeth, but this did not rate a mention in the national press.

After the First World War numbers gradually declined, falling below 100 in 1928, below 50 in the 1960s and reaching an all-time low of 14 in 1972. Much of this drop in numbers is explained by the departure of the miners and then by the opening of the Beacon secondary school in Aspatria in 1964, with the result that all children left the school at the age of eleven instead of just the few who had gained places at the two grammar schools in Wigton. Inevitably, a school with so few pupils was more than once threatened with closure, but, happily, it has survived and now flourishes with 40 on the roll.

Mr Braithwaite, the Headmaster, with his class in 1954. This was the senior class of 11s to 15s. Of the 24 pupils shown only four are girls. There were 74 children on the register in that year. Mr Braithwaite, an energetic Headmaster, had been appointed in 1945. He took parties to the Festival of Britain in 1951, to the Coronation of Queen Elizabeth II in 1953 and in this year to Manchester. The photograph is taken looking west, with Peare Tree House and the Manse just visible on the left.

The Two Wars

On 26 June 1921 the log book of the School's Headmaster, Mr Stephenson, records the unveiling of the War Memorial by his son, Lieut. W. Stephenson. 'The Memorial is rustic in form, stands 9 ft high, is made of Aberdeen red granite, the work having been executed and designed by Messrs Beattie & Son, Carlisle, at a cost of £110.' The dedication ceremony was performed by the Rev. J. Wordsworth. The log book contains a copy of the report in *The West Cumberland Times*, with Lieut. Stephenson's speech. Seven names were inscribed on the stone, four of them being former pupils at the school. Six more names were to be added at the end of the Second World War. The Memorial is still kept in good shape and a service is held there annually to commemorate those who died.

Memories of the First World War are difficult to come by. Apart from the families who mourned the loss of those who died at the front it's probable that Blennerhasset, like most rural communities, suffered few material effects. There is surprisingly little mention of it in the School log books. In 1916 the children contributed 11s.6d to the Overseas Club (for soldiers serving overseas). By this time the school was entirely staffed by women teachers. In September 1918 the whole school spent several days bramble gathering; the weights collected were recorded, the winner being a girl who gathered 12 lb. In all 93 lb. was collected. The next month the school closed down completely for a week for the gathering of the potato crop. These are the only references to any changes which might have been brought about by the war. Much more space is allotted to the serious flooding which twice caused the school to be closed during September 1918. Baggrow was completely cut off, several houses were flooded and the water came up to the school gates.

Much more information is available about the Second World War. Staying with the school log books, we learn that the school was

The Village War Memorial was erected on the base of an old cross that occupied the site in the nineteenth century,

IN
MEMORY AND
HONOUR OF
THE MEN OF
BAGGROW AND
BLENNERHASSET
WHO FELL IN THE
GREAT WAR

1915
HENRY H. BEWLEY
1916
JOHN G. BIRNEY
GEORGE LAWSON
1917
RICHARD REYNOLDS
1918
FRANK SHANKLIN
THOMAS W. BELL
GEORGE TELFORD

+ 1914-18 +

THEY DIED FOR US.

WORLD WAR II
1939-45
IN PROUD
AND AFFECTIONATE
REMEMBRANCE OF THE
FALLEN OF BAGGROW
AND BLENNERHASSET

1940 ALBERT B.SUTTON
STANLEY BATY
1942 FRANCES A.WRAPE
1943 JOHN PATTERSON
1944 ROBERT ELLIOTT
FRED M.ATKINSON

LEST WE FORGET.

closed on 1 September 1939, two days before war was declared, for the Government Evacuation Scheme. When it opened again on 18 September classes were operated in two shifts: 9-12.30 for children from Blennerhasset and South Shields and 1-4.30 for those from Newcastle. In January 1940 the seven evacuees form Newcastle were reallocated to Fletchertown but, this being the period of the 'phoney war', when no bombing occurred, six of them went back home. Then in July 20 more evacuees came from Newcastle, since by this time the bombing had begun in earnest. A few months later the headteacher of their school, Cowgate School in Newcastle, called to see them and 'expressed great surprise and pleasure upon their improved appearance'. At the end of the year each of them received a present of one shilling from Newcastle Education Committee. Those from South Shields did better though: they got ls.9d. By early 1943, when the worst of the bombing seemed to be over, only one evacuee was left from Newcastle and some of those from South Shields failed to come back to the school after the summer holidays.

So much for the evacuees. Other entries in the log book record the putting up of blackout in November 1939, a visit in June 1940 by Gunner John Rumney, who had been rescued from Dunkirk, the receipt of one stirrup pump early in 1941, fortunately never used, and War Weapons Week, also in 1941, when £77.12s.2d. was raised for the School Bank. In the next year gas masks were tested, by what method is not explained, and a Day of Prayer was held at the Social Service Centre. Here too the National Day of Prayer was observed in 1943. Finally two days holiday were granted for the end of the war in Europe. Just before this comes the first and only mention of evacuees from London: three were medically examined before they returned home.

Blennerhasset never suffered from the bombing, but it did experience an aircraft crash, when in 1942 a Royal Air Force plane crashed in a field behind a house near the High Road, killing both its crew. Those who lived in the village at the time all have vivid memories of this tragedy. Also remembered are the army trucks parked all over the village at one point and the soldiers billeted at Brayton Hall, which also had a small airfield in its ground.

This airfield, actually an RAF dispersal station, or Satellite Landing Ground, was opened in May 1942 after lengthy negotiations to close the minor road next to it. It was fenced off from cattle and camouflage was provided by painting dummy hedges across the landing strips. Its function was to enable aircraft to be parked there until they were needed for active service. It was reported that more Wellington bombers were assembled there (over 200) than on any other airfield. At various times Flying Fortresses, Halifaxes and Spitfires were also kept there. When the airfield closed at the end of the war those aircraft which had not been used were transferred to the parent station at Kirkbride.[50]

In this war the rural areas did not fare much better than the towns since food rationing was quickly introduced nationally to cover all the basic necessities. Most commodities seemed to come in quantities of two ounces a week except for cheese, which went down to one ounce. Even bread and potatoes were eventually put on the ration. These measures, although they certainly led to some hardship, did mean that no-one went without, and it turned out in fact that the British population ended the war much healthier than it had begun it. Country people had the advantage that they could supplement their rations from the land. Gardens were turned over to crops and many people had the space to keep hens, ducks and pigs. These activities were also regulated. For every two pigs slaughtered one could be kept and one given 'to the country'. The small meat ration could also be boosted from the very plentiful supply of rabbits in the fields and the River Ellen was, unlike today, rich in trout.

Sport

Sport must have been popular well before the end of the nineteenth century, but the first positive record of any sport taking place in Blennerhasset dates from 1890, when the Cricket Club was founded by Sir Wilfrid Lawson. Matches were played in his own grounds at Brayton Park against various local teams until 1922, when a field in Baggrow began to be used. A new playing field, on the land once known as Hodgson's Croft, was bought and handed to the Parish Council in 1953. It was paid for largely from concerts and donations from the School Fund and was specifically for the use of the two villages of Blennerhasset and Baggrow. But cricket was not played here until 1982, when a pavilion was built on the site.

The game still flourishes, with games played in the Cumbria League and the Carlisle and District League, as well as Under 15 and

Above: The champion rugby team of 1912-13. They were winners of the Cumberland Challenge Cup and Shield. Several men in the team were miners. The gentleman standing fourth from left in the back row, Mr N.Moore, also appears in the cricket photo of 1908 and in the picture of the 1912 Carnival Cricket team.

Above: The cricket team of 1908. and add after 'in 1890'. Matches were then played on the Brayton Park Estate.

Left:
The Blennerhasset and Baggrow Cricket club was founded by Sir Wilfrid Lawson in 1890. The smart fixture list brochure from 1921 suggests that they were still aware of their aristocratic beginnings.

118

Blennerhassett & Baggrow Cricket Club.	
President:- F. J. Thomson, Baggrow House, Baggrow.	

V—Pres;-

Sir W. Lawson. W. Parkin Moore, J.P.,; J. Stephenson. Esq. A. Lawson Esq. R. Moore, Esq. W. Hanvey Esq. Jos Robinson, Esq, T. T. Robinson, Esq T. Pattinson, Esq, T. Miller. Esq. W. P. Robinson, Esq. J. Blacklcck, Esq, J. Reay, Esq. J. C. Robinson. Esq,

Committee:—

Capt............Mr. R. Moore
Ve-Capt ..Mr W. Tweddle
Messrs Jos Sowerby, J Brown
R. Johnston, W. Clemitson
J. B. Clemitson. I. M. Graves
W. Husbands, J. Wilkinson,
Secretarys' & Treasurer.

Fixtures, 1921

Date		Oppt.	Gd	F	A
May	7	Cockermouth	A		
	14	Plumbland	H		
	21	Aspatria & Br	H		
	28	Allhallows	A		
June	4				
	11	Allhallows	H		
	18	Plumbland	A		
	25	Maryport	H		
July	2				
	9				
	16	Workington	H		
	21	Workington	A		
	23	Cockermouth	H		
	30	Dovenby	A		
Aug	6	Asp't'a & Br't	A		
	13	Dovenby	H		
	20	Maryport	A		
	27				

Ground at Baggrow.

Hon Tre— T. B. Charters.

Joint Hon Sects—

R. J. Hanvey & S. Barton.

The Cricket Club's fixtures from 1921. As the two villages ran into each other, most activities were, and still are, shared between them, although Baggrow actually belongs to the parish of Allhallows. Among the names are two Hanveys, father and son, both cobblers. and J.Blacklock, tenant and soon to be owner of the People's Shop.

Under 13 sides playing in the Cumbria Junior League. This is the only sport which has survived in an organised form since its beginnings in the late nineteenth century. Cricket is now played at the school again and the team has competed with great success against a number of local schools.

Association football has always been practised on a casual basis, but, as we have seen, there was a Football club in the early twentieth century and another was founded in the 1950s. This time the players changed in the local pub and activity continued until the

119

mysterious disappearance of the goal nets. School football was also pursued at various times. A football match was held in 1923 as a reward for good attendance and in 1930 the Headmaster recorded regular deliveries of materials for cricket, football, rugby and netball. Football matches were played against local schools in the fifties and sixties. After that the school was too small to raise a team. Rugby on the other hand did very well in the period between the wars. The side won the Rugby Cup and Shield playing local teams such as Bothel, Aspatria and Silloth and one of the players, Bob Hanvey (also the cobbler), played for Cumberland and Westmorland when they won the national championship in 1924 and also played for England.

The minor sports pursued now are mostly centred in Aspatria. Members of the Aspatria and District Flying Club have been flying homing pigeons for at least fifty years. Pigeons are regularly sent to France, from which they return, depleted in numbers, but not enough to discourage the practice. Bowls is also played in Aspatria and there was once an Anglers' Club, but it had to give up in the face of the declining numbers of fish in the river, not helped by a discharge of chemical waste into it a few years ago.

The community is fortunate to have the playing field, situated exactly between the two villages, without threat to its future, save for occasional encroachments from the river when it bursts its banks. Cricket tends to be the main activity here, but there are also facilities for football and other sports. The pavilion is being improved and a children's playground has been set up there.

The Grey Goat

Although the "Goat" lies a few metres outside the township of Blennerhasset, in Allhallows parish, it demands a mention, since it serves the residents of both Baggrow and Blennerhasset, as well as some from further afield. Its age is uncertain but Glenn Stamper, the present publican, kindly showed me the deeds in his possession, which date back to 1779. By her will of that date, Mary Atkinson, who died the following year, left to her son John the houses and orchard "with the Settle Cupboard Grates and Bedstead and a Bedding of Cloaths". After that it rapidly passed through a number of owners, not without complications, including a court case over an unpaid mortgage debt. The matter having been decided in court, the two disputants, William Hodgson and John Kirkup, sold the property in 1814 to James Quin, a blacksmith of Great Broughton, for £520. From James's son, William, a yeoman, it passed to his son-in-law, James Lister, a house carpenter also of Great Broughton, in 1838. So, as with the fields, the Goat seems to have belonged to a series of owners who lived elsewhere and rented it out to others whose names are not recorded.

In 1867 it was still in the hands of the Listers when Mary Lister on her death left it to her son James, who died in 1890, leaving it to his niece Miss Jane Hodgson of Seaton and Miss Mary Ann Norman of Brigham. For the first time we learn the name of the tenant, Jane Charters. The Misses Hodgson and Norman wasted no time and sold it to a brewer, Joseph Dalzell of Whitehaven, for £1,450, and Joseph three years later sold it to his own company, the Parton and Harrington Breweries Limited, for £2,000. From this it looks as though a pub was a better investment at that time than farmland, this being a period of depression for farming.

There is a gap in the records for the early twentieth century but Glenn Stamper, the present owner, kindly provided me with a list of the publicans from about the 1920s, followed in brackets with the landlady, usually the publican's wife, which may be of interest to anyone who remembers them or may have heard tell of them. We begin in the 1920s with the long tenancy of Thomas T.Robinson (helped successively by Martha, possibly his mother, and then by his wife, Jinny); then came David Hamilton (Jean, his wife, the daughter of the Robinsons), who also had the pub for quite a long time, at least twenty years; then Mike Fee (Pat Fee) and Roger Dunant (Trish Dunant). We have now reached the 1980s. It was usual during these years for the landlord to have a full-time job outside the pub. Bob Irving (Carol) and Arthur Wilson (Barbara) followed with short stints And then the pub was relinquished by its owner, the brewer Matthew Brown, who went out of business. It was about to be sold as a private house when it was bought by Trevor and Dorothy Pearson, who modernised it, providing proper toilets and a pool table. From this time on the pub was a Free House. Matthew Greenbank (Susan), who put in a new cellar, John Bayliss (Mary) and Malcolm Gray (Sue) took over for fairly short periods and the pub has flourished under its present owner, Glenn Stamper, for the last six years.

More to be Done

The more research I have done the more I have realised how much there is still to be discovered about the history of this village. I have, for a start, limited myself to Blennerhasset itself, and the story of Kirkland deserves its own history, as does Torpenhow of course. And then I have only covered the last two centuries and it would be fascinating to find out what was happening to the village in earlier times. The Reivers would certainly come into this and the Pele Tower at Harby Brow must have an interesting story to tell. What was happening in the seventeenth century when Blennerhasset was considered prosperous enough to have its own market? When was the cross put up? Can anything be discovered about the village in medieval times? We know who owned it at various times but nothing much more so far.

There are many old houses here which could benefit from their history being looked into. It would be interesting to see some of the people who figure in this book come to life instead of being just names on legal documents. What sort of man was George Dawson? And why did his son fail to make good? How did the middle one of the Hodgsons manage to run up debts of £18,000? What happened to the mysterious Mr Martindale? And there must be a lot of information about more recent people and events which I've failed to pick up.

It's hard to say whether enough information could be gathered to make another book, but there's always the hope that enough could be found. This applies not just to the past but to the village as it is now for the benefit of those who come after us and for whom some of that knowledge will otherwise be lost for ever.

References

References beginning CA refer to archives in the Carlisle Record Office.

1. *Proceedings of the Cumberland and Westmorland Archaeological and Antiquarian Society, 1990*, vol. 90, p.127. The next reference is to the same series, 1956, vol. 55, p.200.

2. *Hints on Agricultural Subjects and on the Best Means of improving the Condition of the Labouring Classes*, J.C.Curwen, Esq., M.P. of Workington Hall, Cumberland, 2nd ed., 1809.

3. CA; Q/Mil

4. CA; PR/138/14 5. CA; PR138/18

6. CA; PR 13 8/ 18

7. Nicolson and Burn, quoted in *North Country Life in the Eighteenth Century, vol.2, Cumberland and Westmorland, 1700-1830,* Edward Hughes, OUP, 1965, p.25.

8. CA; D/LAW/1175

9. CA-- D/LAW/1/61

10. CA; DiLAW/2i 16

11. CA; D/LAW/1/65

12. CA; D/LAW/2/ 16

13. CA; D/LAW/1167

14. CA: D/LAW/8114

15. CA; D/LAW/1/65

16. CA; D/LAW/2/15

17. CA-- D/LAW/1/65

18. CA; D/LAW/1/67

19. CA; DiLAW/ 1 /6 5

20. CA; D/LAW/1/69

21. CA; D/LAW/1170

22. CA D/LAW/1175

23. D L AW/2/ 15

24. V D LAW/1/74

25. CA, D/LAW/1/74

26. *On the Farming of Cumbria,* William Dickinson, from *the Journal of the Royal Agricultural Society of England, 1853,* quoted in *The Farming of Cumbria. A History*, John Burgess, Carlisle,1989, p.37

27. CA; D/LAW/1/75

28. CA; D/LAW/1/67

29. CA; D/LAW/1/68

30, CA: D/LAW/ 1 /67

31. ibid.

32. CA; D/LAW/1/59

33. CA; DILAWI I /61

34. *Cumbrian Villages,* Kenneth Smith, Robert Hale, 1973.

35. Nicolson and Burn, op. cit., p.25.

36. *Ten Years of Gentleman Farming,* William Lawson and Charles Hunter, Hay Nisbet, Printer, Glasgow, n. d. (1874?).

37. CA; PR/138/5-13

38. CA; PR/138/3

39. CA; PR/138115

40. CA; PR/138/3

41. CA; PR/138/56

42. Religious Worship. England and Wales. Report and Tables. London, printed by Geo. E.Eyre and William Spottiswoode for HMSO, 1853.

43. CA; D/LAW/1/51

44. *West Cumberland Coa*l, Oliver Wood, C.W.A.A.S. Extra Series XXIV, 1988.

45. From the minutes of the School Managers and the Log Books of Blennerhasset School for the loan of which I am indebted to the Head Teacher, Mrs Allyson Stevenson.

46. *The Times and Star*, 18.3.2005

47. CA; D/LAW/1/74

48. *History, Directory and Gazetteer of Cumberland, Westmorland with Furness and Cartmel,* Parson and White, 1829. Michael Moon, 1976.

49. *History, Gazetteer and Directory of Cumberland, Mannix and Whellan, 1847.* rep.M.l Moon, 1974.

50. *Action Stations, vol. 3, Military Airfields and the North-West*, David Smith, Patrick Stevens Ltd., 1981.

Books Published by Bookcase

Books can be ordered directly from Bookcase, 19 Castle Street, Carlisle, CA3 8SY, 01228 544560, www.bookscumbria.com. Please add £1 for postage.

A Canny History of Carlisle.   Jim Eldridge. £7.99
Caught on the cusp between England and Scotland, Carlisle has a better story to tell than most cities. Our Canny Historian, Jim Eldridge,creator of Radio 4's King Street Junior, is just the chap to tell the tale of the Great Border City - from the days of the Celts and the Romans right up to the floods and the football team.

Carlisle to Canada: A Family Chronicle.   Cathy Smith   £8.99
Cathy Smith discovered a bundle of old letters in her grandmother's house in Melbourne Road, Carlisle. They told of an Edwardian romance and of emigration to Canada and the parallel lives two families led in Carlisle and on a prairie farm.

The Story of the Newlands Valley.   Susan Grant. £12
Susan Grant's family have lived in the Newlands Valley near Keswick for over 350 years. Her detailed history draws on old records and extensive personal knowledge to paint a picture of a unique isolated community.

Keswick Characters: Volume One   £7.99
The first volume of a series by members of the Keswick Museum telling the life stories of the many eminent and interesting people who have lived in Keswick over the years. This volume includes Sir John Bankes, Jonathan Otley, Joseph Richardson & Sons, Henry Cowper Marshall, John Richardson, George Smith - the Skiddaw Hermit, James Clifton Ward, Hardwicke Drummond Rawnsley, Tom Wilson and Ray McHaffie.

The Wigton Memorial Fountain Solway History Society   £10
In 2004 Solway History Society restored the George Moore Memorial Fountain which stands in the centre of Wigton. This book tells the story of the fountain and of George Moore who built it as a memorial to his wife, Eliza. There is a detailed photographic record of the Fountain itself and a pictorial record of the Fountain through the years.

Strong Lad Wanted For Strong Lass: Growing Up In Carlisle Hunter Davies £8.99

Hunter Davies tells the story of his early years in Carlisle before and after the Second World War. Hunter is one of the country's best known writers and journalists, author of over 30 books.

A New Illustrated History of Wigton   John Higham   £11.50

A detailed, well-researched history spanning nearly two thousand years of this small market town.

Cumberland and Westmorland Wrestling. Roger Robson   £8.95

A modern history of Cumberland and Westmorland wrestling.

Border Television: A History. Mary Scott Parker.   £7.95

A collection of personal memories from the local broadcasters who have been involved in the television station over the years.

A Border Naturalist: The Birds & Wildlife of the Bewcastle Fells & the Gilsland Moors, 1930 - 1966   Ritson Graham   £10.00

A beautifully written study of the rich and varied wildlife in one of the last unspoilt areas of the country.

The Antique County Maps of Cumberland   John Higham.   £11.99

The lavishly illustrated story of the printed maps of Cumberland.

The Anatomy of the Helm Wind. David Uttley. £9.95

A unique study which examines the only named wind in Britain.

Beatys Illustrated Guide to Carlisle   £2.95

A facsimile reprint of the original guide from 1905, first designed to show the Edwardian tourist the finer sights of the flourishing Border city.

The Changing Face of Brampton. Iain Parsons.   £11.50

Over 150 rare photos and a detailed, informative text display the author's affection for this old Cumbrian town.

Provincial Pleasures. Norman Nicholson.   £7.00

A classic account of small town life fifty or more years ago by one of Cumbria's finest writers and poets.

History of Penrith. Ewanian (William Furness)   £7.50

A facsimile reprint of the original edition of 1894, giving a thorough history of Penrith and district up to the end of the nineteenth century.

The Black Angel. Colin Bardgett.   £8.95

A valuable military record. The author has assembled diaries and letters written by men of the Penrith Volunteer Company who went to fight in the Boer War.

Silloth. Mary Scott-Parker.   £8.95
A nostalgic history of this charming Victorian seaside town.

The History of Wigton. Thomas W. Carrick.   £8.95
A facsimile reprint of Carrick's famous work.

Cockermouth Mechanics' Band.   Geoff Hunter.   £7.99
A history of the oldest band in Cumberland, richly illustrated throughout.

The Ghosts of Cumbria. Laurie Kemp.   £6.99
Laurie Kemp has ventured fearlessly among the lakes and fells to uncover the stories of the uneasy spirits that lurk in dark and eerie houses.

The Loving Eye and Skilful Hand: The Keswick School of Industrial Arts.   Ian Bruce.   £15.00
This is the first detailed study of the Keswick School. Founded by the Rawnsleys, the school became one of the most important centres of the Arts and Crafts movement.   The book should be of great interest to historians and collectors.

Hurry, Hurry, While Stocks Last. Hunter Davies.   £7.95
A sideways look at the economic, social and shopping history of Cumbria as seen through local advertisements 1850-1940. Hunter Davies traces the changes in Cumbrian life, in attitudes and activities, trends and fashions.

A Year At Ambleside: Harriet Martineau At Ambleside   Harriet Martineau; Barbara Todd   £10.00
Includes the first UK publication of A Year at Ambleside *by the great Victorian thinker and feminist Harriet Martineau.*

The Carlisle Floods: One Story. Martin Daley. £7.99
After the great Carlisle flood of January 2005 Martin and Wendy Daley had to watch day by day as their home was taken apart and then reconstructed.

Gretna's Secret War. Gordon L. Routledge.   £7.95
In 1915 the greatest munitions factory on Earth was built at Gretna.

Carlisle Cathedral History.   David W.V. Weston   £14.95
The first detailed account of how the Cathedral buildings have developed and changed over the centuries. The closely illustrated text provides a comprehensive record of a wonderful building.

Longtown. Gordon L. Routledge. £11.95

Longtown, the last town in England, was an important crossing point on the River Esk on the border between Scotland and England. This scrapbook of the town, its history and people is an affectionate celebration of a unique place

Carlisle and its Villages. Vincent White. £11.95

An attractive collection of pen and ink drawings of old buildings in and around Carlisle. Vincent White began making these pictures as he saw familiar sights being demolished before his eyes.

Murder in Cumbria. Ian Ashbridge. £8.95

Ian Ashbridge researches the murders that have been committed in the beautiful county of Cumbria in the twentieth century.

Keswick: The Story of a Lake District Town. George Bott. £15

This elegant history tells the story of Keswick from the time of Castlerigg Stone Circle to the present day. Keswick has an importance far beyond its size. German miners came in Elizabethan times, the pencil was discovered here, it was a key centre of the Romantic revolution and later the town became famous for the Keswick Convention.